Voice Over Acting

How to Become a Voice Over Actor

By: Discover Press

Table of Contents

Foreword 4

Introduction 7

Chapter One 10

Chapter Two 17

Chapter Three 33

Chapter Four 46

Chapter Five 50

Chapter Six 57

Final Thoughts 63

What Is Not Covered in This Guide 66

Summary 67

Foreword

This Guide is dedicated to all the voiceover professionals and trainers mentioned in this book, and to all those voiceover actors and talent who make their living in this exciting, creative, and fun field.

We are all, always, standing on the shoulders of giants. Whether you consider yourself to be walking in the footsteps and under the protection of wise and courageous ancestors or whether you see yourself as building on the progress of those who traveled before you, the journey to becoming a voiceover actor is guided by the lessons of talented others.

You walk in the footsteps of Don LaFontaine, who made it his business to mentor and encourage the next generation of voice actors. You travel the path of James Earl Jones, Cree Summer, Eartha Kitt,[1] Whoopi Goldberg, and others who opened doors and expanded opportunities for a diverse new group of voiceover actors.[2] You will, no doubt, light the way for others yourself: break new ground and set a new course based on your unique gifts, lived-life experience, and perspective.

The voiceover business is highly competitive. The pool of talented performers continues to grow in response to technological advances that increase opportunities for more people to work in the business remotely from home. This growth in the pool of available talent coincides with exponential growth in available opportunities for work on a wide variety of projects. Voice actors are needed for voice enabled virtual assistants, phone systems, automated products and services, and an ever-expanding number of household appliances, gadgets, and toys. These new opportunities mirror growth in commercial, animation, gaming, corporate communications, training, and film and video work. As more communications platforms come online you can expect the growth in opportunity in the field to continue.

Yet despite the growth in opportunity, it can be more difficult to succeed. The increase in the size of the talent pool can worsen the problem. How does a voiceover actor learn about, let alone get their name out to, all the producers and companies that might want to hire them? How can you stand out among the best and consistently book the best projects and jobs? The goal of this Guide is to provide you with some answers to these questions.

---

[1] See also: https://youtu.be/ol9G4f6Wxec
[2] "As Audiobook Market Grows, Narrators of Color Find Their Voice - The New York Times."

In my research, I have been impressed by the generosity of so many people who have been willing to share their insights despite the highly competitive nature of the work. These people have shared the benefits of their experience, guidance, training, and tips for success. The amount of free, good, and excellent information available on the internet and in books is amazing and quite literally overwhelming. You can find free tutorials, free training and advice, and an abundance of encouragement.

My goal has been to search through much of what is accessible to provide you with an accurate synthesis of the best information available. Most of what I am providing to you is not unique to my way of thinking. I am providing what I have gleaned from others—with attribution. This Guide seeks to compile what exists collectively over decades of experience and training.

Even so, I cannot promise that I have identified every resource available to you. However, I do believe that I have found key resources and provided you with the information that you will need to dig further.

This Guide should give you a solid foundation of information and prompt you to search for more. In the end, only you can do what is necessary for you to succeed. The ongoing effort to continue to learn and improve is at the heart of the voiceover profession.

So, standing on the shoulders of the giants who have gone before us and with the benefit of the wisdom and insight of so many generous people in this field, I offer you *A Guide to Starting Your Career in Voiceover* and wish you well on your journey. Welcome to the life of creative entrepreneurship.

A Note about Ableism

As I wrote this Guide, I was troubled by the idea that the suggested techniques for learning about the voiceover business might be seen to exclude some people. This is particularly true of the section on using your ear, and my description of the ear as the most important tool. It is true that many will interact with voiceover work through hearing. However, I have no doubt that as technology evolves, more will participate in the work and be reached without hearing it. The opportunity to be a voiceover actor is not limited to people with hearing. Deaf people can and will adapt the ideas and tools described here to develop new techniques. The support for this belief can be found easily in the artistic fields of dance, theatre and film, and many other fields beyond those. Similarly, non-sighted people can read voiceover scripts.

If anyone feels that they are not included in this Guide, please know that it is not my intent.

What is at work is only the limits of my imagination and ***not yours***.

Introduction

Let me guess—you have been toying with the idea of working as a voiceover actor for some time. Maybe you are already an actor looking for new or additional opportunities for work. Maybe you are not an actor, but you have been told you have a good voice. You are wondering whether this is the time to give it a try.

Maybe you have already given voiceover work a try—well, sort of. You have searched around the internet and watched some videos on YouTube, but you can't quite picture yourself in a recording booth. Maybe you even bought a microphone, downloaded some recording software, and converted your bedroom closet into a tiny, hot, sweaty recording studio—wait, that would be me.

Maybe you have not auditioned for a voiceover role in some time. What if your voiceover credits are so old that you barely remember what it was that you did?

More people are working from home. Working from a home studio, on your own schedule, and with the opportunity to better balance home and family, is extremely attractive. Whatever your background and experience with voiceover, or your reason for wanting to take a closer look now, if your goal is to move from a tantalizing fantasy to reality, you need to immerse yourself in the vast amount of information about the voiceover business that is available. Moving from the *idea* of being a voiceover actor to becoming a booked and paid voiceover actor is not easy. You need a plan. You need discipline to work the plan.

My Approach: Theory *and* Practice

This Guide will provide a big picture vision *and* practical, tangible ways to operationalize that vision. I will get you started and headed in the right direction.

Finishing will be up to you. No one person and no guide can guarantee your success. I will give you my best advice. Think of this Guide as a conversation between you and your best friend. You have shared your quiet dream to become a voiceover actor. You are asking for their best advice. Your friend has traveled some ways down this path and agrees to share the benefit of their experience and research with you. Like a friend, this Guide strives to provide the advice that I would follow myself. And like you, my career and success are important to me.

There is so much good information available on starting a voiceover business: books, internet blogs, and websites created by people with exceptional experience and talent in the voiceover business. The advice provided in this Guide draws heavily from their insights. Reference materials at the end of this Guide allow you to find these experts and delve more deeply into their thinking and approach to the work.

The Guide should give you a jumpstart on your dream and be a time-saver. It provides an overview of the business—the available opportunities and the foundation for understanding what it takes to be successful in voiceover. My goal is to make you a smart consumer of the massive amount of available information and to help you build your career.

So, you want to be a voiceover actor. Congratulations. You have just taken your first step.

How This Guide Is Structured

The Guide starts with an overview of the voiceover business. It then describes a set of tools that are essential to a voiceover talent's career. After describing the tools, the Guide suggests practical ways to master the tools and use them in your long-term plan. At the end of each chapter, and at the end of the Guide, I summarize the information discussed and remind you of key points.

Finally, I will identify some important topics beyond the scope of this Guide. These will be aspects of starting a voiceover business that you should consider and learn more about.

How to Use This Guide

There are several ways to use this Guide. If you are 100% new to voiceover, I would recommend reading through the Guide, or at least scanning it, from beginning to end. Once you have a general overview of the material, you should go back and work your way through each chapter at your own pace. I recommend having a journal handy or some other place where you can make notes.

If you already have some experience and have done research of your own, you can scan the Table of Contents to identify where there is new information of interest to you. You can also turn directly to the resources listed at the end of the Guide, and use them to organize your own research. You might choose to simply read the summary and key points at the end of each chapter. You might just focus on the sections or chapters where there are gaps in your knowledge.

Finally, you can use the Guide as a reference tool. The Guide includes:
*   links to websites with examples of voiceover work and training and resource materials,
*   a Glossary,
*   a Study Outline,
*   a sample planning budget and template, and
*   information about experts you should know and learn more about.

However you plan to use this Guide, I recommend that you create a workplan. Your workplan should have clear objectives, deliverables, and timelines that include how you will use this Guide. This is critical. If you want to make an extraordinary change and addition to your life, you must make a plan that is actionable, tangible, and specific. Reading this Guide is just one part of the work.

Key Takeaways

A successful voiceover business is hard work. There is more to a successful voiceover career than having a microphone, a nice voice, and reading copy.

If you feel energized and motivated after reading this Guide, and you can see yourself working a plan to reach your dream, the voiceover business might be right for you. It is my hope that this Guide will prepare you to meet the necessary challenges ahead and be successful.

Success is not guaranteed; the goal here is to set you on the right path.

We're rolling! (That is voiceover jargon for "let's get started.")

Chapter One

Overview: The Business

The Voiceover Business Today

When most people think about the voiceover business, they usually think about a narrow slice of the available opportunities. We might imagine ourselves as that trusted voice of an insurance company, the seductive intonation of the latest car, or the announcer for the next blockbuster movie. If we think a little more broadly, we might consider the opportunities in audiobooks or animation and gaming. There are many ways in which you can work successfully in the voiceover business. The voiceover industry is growing and with the right approach, you will be positioned to take full advantage.[3]

I am going to describe the range of voiceover opportunities available.[4] As you read through this chapter, you may want to take notes about your initial reaction to a particular type of voiceover work. It can be something as simple as jotting down your gut feeling about the work being described. For example: "fun," "seems boring," "seems interesting," or "don't get it." You might also note information that surprises you. Your notes will be important later when you decide where you first want to focus your voiceover business.

The following are the main sectors of the voiceover business:

- Commercial Market
- Animation and Gaming
- Explainers
- Audiobooks
- Corporate Narration
- Promos
- Radio/Podcast ID
- Looping/ADR Dubbing

---

[3] See more detailed and granular descriptions of the Voiceover market: "2019 Voice-over Industry Report | Voice-Over Freelance."; "2017 Voice Over Trends Report | Voices.Com."; "2017 Global Voice Over Market Report | Voices.Com."

[4] See: How to Start Doing Voice-over Work: https://youtu.be/QCcWs0Y6WCs

- Gadget/Product VO
- Movie Trailers
- IVR Systems Phone Casting/Store Casting
- Voice Matching

Commercial Market

The commercial segment of the voiceover business is that segment of the market where voice talent and actors read copy[5] that sells, informs, persuades, or promotes a product, information, political perspectives, or community and social events. Commercial voiceover is featured on television, radio, the Internet—wherever people seek to reach the public to advertise a product, idea, or event. According to the website Gravyforthebrain.com, an experienced commercial voiceover actor can earn \$250-\$350 for a 30-second major-market commercial, and \$35 for a radio spot in a small market.[6]

The commercial market is what comes to mind when most people think of voiceover work. We think about iconic voice actors and the brands associated with them. We dream of taking our place among them in the pantheon of popular culture. We imagine the income and prestige of having a famously recognizable voice.

The commercial voiceover market is no longer limited to New York City and Los Angeles. While it is true that many national advertisers rely on these creative entertainment hubs to find talent, more opportunities have opened for regional work. The increase in regional opportunities for voiceover work is a positive development because national commercial voiceover work is highly competitive. National advertisers usually hire well-known talent and celebrities. This preference makes it difficult for newcomers to get booked. Regional work is accessible to most people who are not based in New York City or Los Angeles. Regional work provides the opportunity for voiceover newcomers to be big fish in a small pond.

Animation and Gaming

Opportunities to work in the animation and gaming segment of the voiceover industry have expanded exponentially. The video game industry is one of the fastest growing sectors in the U.S.

---

[5] A script.

[6] "How Much Do Voice Actors Make - Factors You Need To Know."; According to Voiceover.com you can earn from \$100 for a regional commercial to \$10,000 for a national TV commercial. "How Much Money Does a Voice Actor Make? | Beginners Guide to Voice Acting | Voices.Com." See also SAG-AFTRA rate sheet.

economy—which is great for voiceover work.[7] Animation and gaming projects are among the most consistent and lucrative sectors of the voiceover business. Voiceover actors bring life to one or more characters in video games or animated productions. Animation voiceover is among the most popular points of entry for newcomers to the industry.[8] According to Voices.com, animation voiceover actors can earn between $100 for 15 seconds of work to $10,000 for a lead role.[9]

Animation and gaming voiceover actors create three-dimensional characters in a two-dimensional world. In addition to creating characters, voice actors provide the sounds and textures for the worlds their characters inhabit. Voiceover actors make the sounds for footsteps, crashes, creaky floors, and galloping horses. These projects, especially gaming jobs, can turn into long-term engagements because of updates and sequels.

Animation and gaming talent usually voice more than one character. For example, the Simpsons' six main cast members voice more than 250 characters[10] collectively. Some animation and gaming voiceover actors also work in front of a green screen on motion capture. Actor and singer Merle Dandridge, known for her role as Grace in *Greenleaf*, among other outstanding performances, does both voiceover and motion capture work. In 2016 she won the BAFTA games award for *"Everybody's Gone to Rapture."*[11]

Each type of voiceover work presents its own set of challenges and benefits. Animation and gaming work can be physically taxing. Industry professionals and SAG-AFTRA have focused on this problem and taken steps to protect voice actors working in this part of the business.[12]

Audiobooks

According to the National Audio Publishers Association, "U.S. audiobook sales in 2019 totaled 1.2 billion dollars," representing a 16% increase in sales over previous years.[13] The level of sales

---

[7] "2017 Global Voice Over Market Report | Voices.Com."
[8] "2017 Global Voice Over Market Report | Voices.Com.";"2019 Voice-over Industry Report | Voice-Over Freelance."
[9] "How Much Money Does a Voice Actor Make? | Beginners Guide to Voice Acting | Voices.Com."
[10] These 6 Actors Voice over 250 Characters: https://youtu.be/SPfdpQTSqls
[11] "Merle Dandridge | Official Website."
[12] https://www.facebook.com/ToddCFrankel, "In $25 Billion Video Game Industry, Voice Actors Face Broken Vocal Cords and Low Pay." Like many other segments in our society, voiceover animation and gaming are also reexamining their approach to casting and increasing opportunities for a larger number of diverse voice talent. See "How Voice Actors Are Fighting Whitewashing in Animation - Vox."
[13] Cobb, "AUDIOBOOKS CONTINUE THEIR MARKET RISE WITH 16% GROWTH IN SALES."

and trajectory for increased sales has held steady. The increased sales likely reflect more demand and more available books in audio format.

The audience for audiobooks has expanded since 1932 when the American Federation for the Blind first recorded "books on tape" for the visually impaired.[14] The production of audiobooks has expanded with its audience. Audiobooks have come a long way, too, from those early days when the Library of Congress was practically alone in producing audiobooks and set the gold standard for recordings. Today the market includes Amazon and its company, Audible; RBmedia, Apple Books, and Storytel.

Amazon's Audible boasts over 200,000 titles.[15] Amazon's ACX platform connects voiceover talent with authors and publishers who want to create audiobooks. These audiobooks can then be sold on the Audible platform.[16] They say they have "2,687 titles open for auditions, 267,989 producers to choose from, and 219,414 audiobooks on sale at Audible, Amazon, and iTunes."[17] Platforms such as ACX provide a great entry point for less experienced audiobook talent as well as experienced voiceover actors. With home studios becoming more prevalent, more people are now able to participate in the audiobook market. Audiobook work takes enormous discipline and stamina to create a high-quality product. You can spend hours in your recording studio reading long passages of text. Websites such as ACX also require you to professionally produce your recorded book. This adds another level of complexity and skill to working in the audiobook industry.

Corporate Narration

Corporate narration includes company training videos and marketing and promotional materials. Voice talent read scripts that on-board new hires, provide instruction on core competencies, and describe the capabilities of new products. According to the 2017 Voiceover Trends report by Voices.com,[18] 18% of the voiceover work completed globally is for business. Corporate narration represents slightly over 24% of the dollar share in North America. It makes up nearly 14% globally, excluding North America. The dollar value of corporate narration is increasing faster than in other jobs.[19] Corporate narration is particularly well suited to building regional and local

---

14 "Audiobooks Market Size, Share | Industry Report, 2020-2027."
15 "The Best Audible Books in 2020 | TechRadar."
16 "Videos | Audiobook Creation Exchange Blog (ACX)."
17 "ACX."
18 "2017 Global Voice Over Market Report | Voices.Com."
19 "2017 Global Voice Over Market Report | Voices.Com.": https://joecipriano.com/

voiceover businesses. A smart, well-researched business plan and disciplined implementation can literally pay dividends in a robust client base with repeat and long-term opportunities.

Promos

Promos are short films, videos, or radio spots used to advertise products or events. These ads are usually two minutes or less. When you watch television or listen to the radio and an upcoming special or the next episode of your favorite program is advertised, you are listening to a voiceover promo. Here is an interesting podcast interview with Joe Cipriano,[20] legendary voiceover talent (and coach), about promos.

Radio and Podcast ID

While listening to your radio or podcast, someone interrupts your groove to tell you what radio station or podcast you are listening to. That voiceover talent could be you. On-air hosts sometimes record radio and podcast identification spots themselves. However, radio stations will often hire specialized voiceover actors. Radio and podcast IDs are generally recorded in blocks. Radio and podcast ID work can lead to long-term employment and repeat work, especially if your voice becomes associated with the station or podcast's brand.

Looping ADR Dubbing

ADR stands for Automated Dialog Replacement. Filmmakers use ADR to record dialogue after the scene has been filmed. ADR is used when the setting or location of a scene prevents high-quality audio from being recorded. Sometimes groups of voiceover actors are hired and work together on ADR for a scene. The ADR group adds background conversation and other sounds to scenes that were pantomimed by background actors when the scene was originally filmed.

Think about a scene being filmed in a train station. Normally hundreds of people would be talking and milling around. If a scene were filmed in a real train station with hundreds of background actors speaking normally, the sound would be too loud to hear the dialogue between the principal actors. Looping ADR dubbing allows the filmmaker to record realistic background sounds after filming. You can hear an excellent interview with Kalathara and Wolfie Trausch of Loop Group

---

[20] "Everything You Need to Know About Promo Voiceover Work."

West. They created their own looping ADR business.[21] This type of work on films and television is most likely available in the vicinity of New York, Los Angeles, Atlanta, and Albuquerque.[22]

Gadget and Product Voiceover

We are surrounded by gadgets, products, and virtual assistants that talk to us, answer questions, find our music, remind us of appointments, and order more gadgets for us. The increasing number of these talking appliances has created new opportunities for voiceover talent. Artificial intelligence is becoming ubiquitous in our lives. As the technology becomes more sophisticated, the need for natural, lifelike voices increases. These new opportunities are a great fit for voiceover actors.[23]

Movie Trailers

Movie trailers come easily to mind when we consider voiceover work. Who can forget the spark of excitement you feel when you hear, "Coming to a theatre near you"? Don LaFontaine's iconic "In A World" trailer openings made him famous as much as or more than the films he promoted. Legends such as Don LaFontaine[24] and Hal Douglas[25] have become synonymous with this aspect of voiceover work. Unfortunately, movie trailer jobs may be among the most difficult roles to secure. Film promoters and advertisers tend to rely on a small pool of celebrity and well-known voices. Movie trailers are an unlikely place for newcomers to start in the industry. This Guide, which is designed for beginners and those with less experience, will not focus on movie trailers. However, you can learn more from voiceover actor Thompson Howell's book, *Movie Trailer Master: Complete Voiceover*. He has designed a training program as well.[26]

IVR Systems Phone Casting

IVR systems phone casting stands for Interactive Voice Response systems. IVR systems are the persistently cheerful voice on the other end of your phone. They screen your question before sending your call to the appropriate representative or customer service agent. This workflow often

---

[21] "(59) Voicing for the Background | Film Jobs with Loop Group West - YouTube.": https://youtu.be/BO1ivoU8GDc
[22] "4 of the Best Cities for Film and TV Production Crews | Casting Agencies Directory."
[23] "Why Your Next Voiceover Job Is Probably in Your Phone."
[24] See: https://donlafontaine.com/
[25] https://donlafontaine.com/; See also: https://uncrate.com/video/hal-douglas-a-great-voice/
[26] "Movie Trailer Mastery | Complete Voiceover." See also: Thompson, "In a World without Voiceovers." See: "Women Narrate Movie Trailers | Industry News - Celebrities | Voices.Com Blog" for additional insight into this segment of the voiceover business.

requires the voice talent to record a single line at a time, called prompts. An IVR systems voiceover actor generally records a block of prompts. Clients are billed for each prompt based upon an agreed upon price and usually an additional fee. [27]

Voice Matching

Voice matching is a subset of ADR work. ADR is used when voiceover actors or talent record copy that imitates a celebrity voice. ADR is used for branded dolls and action figures. ADR might also be used when the dialogue in film must be recorded and the original actor is unavailable.[28]

Chapter Summary/Key Takeaways

The voiceover business is evolving and growing quickly. Voiceover work can provide exciting opportunities for a diverse talent pool in a wide variety of locations. While some technical aspects of voiceover work are the same, each type of work requires its own skillset and style.

Now that you have a general overview of the voiceover business, it is time to learn about the tools you will use to start and enhance your voiceover career.

The next chapter will discuss the most important tool for voiceover work. You will be surprised by which tool it is—your *ear*.

---

[27] See: "IVR Voice Over Jobs - Create An Income By Voicing IVR." "The Importance of IVR Phone System Voice Over | Voices.Com Blog."
[28] See: "Voice Matching in Movies - Business Insider."

Chapter Two

Identify Your Tools: Your Ear

"On a cold January morning, a Grammy award-winning violin virtuoso put on a baseball cap, took out his $3.5 million Stradivarius violin and went to work. Apart from several strikingly perceptive toddlers, few people stopped to listen to this extraordinary artist play six classical pieces. After he had played for 45 minutes, passersby had contributed a total of $31.

Just the other day, this same artist had filled a concert hall where tickets sold for $100 a seat. No one recognized the extraordinary gift they were being given on that day."[29]

Several moral conclusions can be drawn from this experiment sponsored by the Washington Post: people are too busy, stressed, and self-absorbed to stop and notice beauty when they encounter it. We are so unaccustomed to true beauty that we do not recognize it. People ignore beauty when it shows up in unexpected places.

This story makes the point that we must take the time to notice the subtle artistry in voiceover work. We must take the time especially when we find it in the most mundane of surroundings.

You must develop your ear to hear the artistry in the work of other voiceover actors. When you study and understand the skill and technique that goes into telling a story naturally in the most unnatural of settings, you will have unlocked the secret of voiceover success.

Identify Your Tools: Train Your Ear[30]

Your ear is your most important asset in the voiceover business. It is more important than your voice.

---

[29] "Grammy-Winning Violinist Joshua Bell Delights Masses at DC Subway Concert | PBS NewsHour."
[30] Great Resource overall: https://youtu.be/Q9SFX3qGhQA Audio Narrator Tips & Tricks: How to Sound Conversational, Christopher Romance – Excellent description with a meter charter describing the "push & pull" quality of the various types of voiceover compared to film and theatre acting.

Wait a minute. What? I will say it again: your ear is more important than having the most beautiful, melodious timbre to your voice. When you think about it, it makes sense.

While you might be blessed with the physicality of flexible vocal cords that can produce warm tones, that gift does not guarantee success as a voiceover actor. You must also know how to use your natural gift to tell a compelling story. You do not actually need an exceptional voice to be a voiceover actor. The most important thing is that you can use whatever vocal instrument you have been given, and strike the proper tone to be persuasive to your target audience. Your well-trained ear is an essential tool in this. If you listen and practice, you will soon be able to produce the desired effect. You will know when *you hit the proper notes* to tell a convincing story for your client, their customers, and constituency.

Start by listening and learning what to expect from an excellent voiceover performance.

For what should you be listening? While there are common elements of high-quality voiceover work across genres, there will be some techniques that will be specific to each.

Commercial Voiceover

The key to a great commercial voiceover performance is expressing a clear point of view. The listener should be able to hear and to answer the following questions based on your performance:

> ➤ Where are you?
> ➤ Who are you talking to?
> ➤ What do you want them to do?

A point of view:

If you do not have a clear picture of where you are, who you are talking to, and what you want or what you want somebody to feel, you will just be a disembodied voice reading some words that have no impact.

A voiceover performance is commonly called a "read." However, successful voiceover talent must do a lot more than simply "read" the copy or script. The best voiceover presents a point of view. It allows the listener to imagine where you are and what you are doing when they hear you speak. If you want your audience to know "where you are, what you are doing, and to whom you are speaking," then you, the voice actor, must know these things first, yourself.[31]

---

[31]See: *HAGEN, UTA, FRANKEL, HASKEL, & MASTERS, ANGELE. (2014). Respect for Acting. Brilliance Audio.*

Can you close your eyes and imagine that the voice actor is standing in front of a warm stove, offering you a taste of freshly baked lasagna? Can you imagine being tempted to sneak a first bite? Could the voice actor instead be speaking to a partner or grandchild? Are they sitting at the kitchen table? Are they tasting the food as they have a heart-to-heart chat?

If you have had formal acting training, preparing to answer these questions for your voiceover role will be part of your normal routine. The challenge here is that once you have answered these questions in your head, you must learn to use only your voice and breath to convey the answers.

I will discuss the technical aspects of analyzing copy again and in more detail later in this Guide, but here are some initial thoughts to keep in mind.

Suppose you booked a commercial for a new down jacket with the following copy:

> *Cold weather is approaching, and you and your family had better be ready. It is time to make sure your family has what it needs to face even the worst weather. But having the right winter gear takes money.*
>
> *Never2Frosty coats are the perfect solution. Warm, affordable, and shipped to you free.*

Read the copy above. Take a deep breath and read it out loud without thinking. The copy itself is not particularly compelling. That may well be the case for much of the copy you are asked to perform. Now record yourself on your phone reading the copy—no preparation, just read aloud. Now *listen* to the recording. How does it sound? Silly? Unconvincing?

This time, take a deep breath and imagine that you are talking on the phone to a relative with small children living in Boston. Record yourself reading the copy again, remembering what it felt like to be talking to that relative. Does the recording sound any different? How is it different?

Now, imagine that you are outside on a chilly morning visiting with a neighbor. Record yourself reading the copy again and listen to it. Does it sound different from earlier recordings? Each read that you recorded should sound, and therefore *feel,* different to you. You are training your ear to listen for and hear "point of view."

Who are you?

To drill down on the idea of point of view a little more, voiceover professionals and coaches urge voiceover actors to pick a type or a character. Anna Garduno of Voice Forward[32] encourages people to come up with characters or their type and give that character a name.

For example: How would the copy sound if the person speaking were: "the nosy neighbor," the "know-it-all" at work, or the shy person at a party? Decide who you are or who your character is more than simply identifying your "type" or personality. Your decision must be guided by who your target audience is and what you want them to do. You should ask yourself, who would influence your target audience most? Who would they most like to hear from? Who will most likely get the reaction or response that your voiceover client seeks?

Fortunately, your voiceover client will likely be able to provide you with answers to these questions about their audience. If they do not volunteer this information, you should ask. If they have not thought about these questions, be prepared to help them think over and answer these questions with them. Then it will be up to you to reach into your bag of voiceover skills to bring out the character as you work with the script. As you gain more experience, you will learn how to quickly match your internal cast of characters to your client's objectives and bring those characters to life in the script.

When we "get practical" later in the Guide, I will identify ways to train your ear to hear when voice actors succeed and fail to deliver a point of view in their performance.

Animation and Gaming

For animation and gaming, the focus is on creating a character and telling a long form story through that character.[33] Sometimes the voiceover talent will be given a complete script. This provides the voice actor with important information about the story and arc of the narrative. Having the complete script makes it easier to understand character development and the way in which relationships between characters evolve.

However, often animation and gaming voiceover actors only receive partial scripts. The script may be written on the spot or through collaborative improvisation. The voiceover actor may not know how the story ends when they begin the project. Sometimes voiceover talent receives the script a few pages at a time. They might be given sentences or words to read that seem random. Here is where training and experience will pay off. Whether you are working from a fully animated film

---

[32] "About Voice Forward & Anna Garduno."
[33] "How to Master Voiceover Character Skills."

script or a series of lines for a video game, you must create a well-rounded character embodied with your voice.

The process will be much the same as creating a character or type for commercial voiceover. It will be much the same as creating a character for film or on stage. For animation projects, the artist's drawings can provide clues that will help with character development. Other times the animation artist will take their cues from you and your physical impression of the role. Your job then is to figure out how to reflect your understanding of the character in the voice. You are painting an auditory picture of the character. You must think about the sound of their speech, how they breathe, and the sounds they make moving through space.

Animation and gaming voiceover work is most like traditional acting. You will be able to use many of the methods you normally would use to create a character for a movie or on stage.

Your preparation might include answering the following questions:

- What information can you glean about the character from any narrative or introduction?
- What does the character say about herself?
- What is her goal?
- What does she want in the scene or segment you are taping, and from whom?
- What do others want from her?
- What do others say about her?
- If she were an animal or inanimate object, what would she be?
- How would she stand, sit, or walk into a room?

When you answer these questions, you will be able to build characters from the ground up. To the extent that the script is not finished, or information is not available, fill in gaps yourself.

Now that you have the character in mind, speak. How does the character's posture and carriage affect your voice? When this character is placed in a specific time and place, how does your voice change? How does your character sound if they are a wizard living in a cramped, drafty cottage?

How well and completely do the contours of the character come across in the voice?

Corporate Narration: Explainer Videos[34]

Explainer videos are a segment of the corporate narration market. These 90-second-or-less videos are designed to boost sales or conversion rates for a product or service. They describe a function or service in detail. Explainer videos can be found on the landing page of a company or organization website. These videos may be animated or live action and might include interactive infographics or white boards to illustrate key points and messages.

The voiceover talent's role[35] is to deliver the message and information in an engaging way, designed to grab and hold the audience's attention. The voice actor should learn as much as possible about the prospective audience for the video. You must know the audience and what your client wants from them to match your voiceover performance to the task.

Listen to the voiceover work for corporate narration or explainer videos. Ask yourself the following questions:

- What is the voice actor doing to grab and hold the audience's attention?
- How does the voice actor use the pace, pitch, and volume?
- How is the voice used to emphasize important information and help the audience remember it?

Marketing strategist Lisa Isbell wrote on the blog Hubspot.com[36] to provide an overview of explainer videos. She lists seventeen explainer videos which she considers the best. Of note in her article is Explainer #4 by Yum Yum videos. Explainer #4 describes the variety of explainer videos than can be tailored to meet many businesses' objectives. Lisa Isbell's article is particularly interesting and useful because it is written from the perspective of the client or company that might hire you. It provides good insight into their perspective and their challenges.

Audiobooks present a variety of opportunities for voiceover projects. Well-known authors and novice writers use platforms such as Audible to reach a wide range of audiences.

Audiobook voiceover is challenging. It requires physical stamina, a mastery of language, and the ability to shift dialogue between characters seamlessly. At the same time, the characters

---

[34] For more information on how to get work in this area, listen to the Podcast from VO School on Backstage: "How to Find Voiceover Work in E-Learning, Corporate Narration, Audiobooks + Explainer Videos."
[35] For additional insight for working with voiceover in the corporate narrative setting see:"7 Tips for Working with Voice-Over in Corporate Video Projects."
[36] "17 Examples of Fabulous Explainer Videos."

themselves and the interactions between characters must not detract from the flow of the narrative or the story being told.

In addition to the skill with which characters are rendered, you should listen for:

- Clear and careful articulation of words and a pace that engages the audience
- A steady pace that carries through for the duration of the book
- A sense of the story's arc that comes from careful, thorough preparation (to be discussed more in the section on "the read")
- An appropriate quality of voice and mood—a sense of intimacy
- A natural or conversational tone

Promo[37]

Voiceover for promos is a fast-paced, brief interaction with the audience.

When you listen to high quality promos, you should be able to answer the following questions:

- Is the voice unique and memorable? What do you remember most?
- Does the promo tell you something about the brand? What?
- Does the promo tell you what brought the voiceover actor to the brand? What?
- Does the promo grab your attention? What grabbed your attention?

It is worth noting that unlike commercial, animation, or gaming, the emphasis in voiceover for promos is *not on building character*. The emphasis is on *grabbing the attention of the target audience and leaving a memorable impression*. Creating a "type" or "character" comes into play only in so much as it helps to grab the audience's attention and create an impression.

Radio/Podcast ID[38]

I think about radio and podcast ID voiceover as a subset of promo work. These projects open podcasts and announce the radio station's identification. You are listening here for memorability and personality that matches the brand of the radio station or podcast. In addition to listening for the answers to the questions for promos, listen for clarity.

---

[37] "Everything You Need to Know About Promo Voiceover Work."
[38] "Podcast Voice Overs - Pro Podcast Solutions."

Looping/ADR Dubbing, Voice Matching[39]

ADR is used to record or rerecord dialogue for a scene. Filmmakers use ADR to overcome obstacles to obtain clear audio and high-quality sound. In addition to reading lines from a script, the voice actor might add such sounds as grunts, laughing, coughing, or screaming to the audio track. Sometimes groups or teams of voiceover actors add background chatter to scenes in films.

It is important to be able to replicate the quality and timbre of the original actor's voice when voice matching. When you analyze looping/ADR dubbing and voice matching, you will be listening for how seamlessly the background conversations and dialogue work in the film or video. The unremarkable nature of the voiceover performance will be the hallmark of excellence and demonstration of the skill required. Said another way, if your attention is drawn to the background conversations in a scene, that is an example of what not to do. You should not be able to tell that dialogue has been dubbed or replaced. Listen for whether the energy and level of passion in the scene is matched by the voiceover performance.

Gadget/Product VO, IVR Systems Phone Casting/Store Casting

Because here you are not really telling a story, you will be listening for clarity, voice quality, and pace. Oftentimes voiceover projects involving products and phone systems are taking the audience through a series of steps. You will want to listen here to see whether you can identify the techniques the voice talent is using to ensure the audience follows the proper steps in the correct sequence.

Get Practical: How to Do It

Now that you have an overview of the business and some of its technical and artistic features, you can train your ears to listen for three things:

1) To recognize the best examples of each type of voiceover work,

2) To recognize the specific techniques being used to achieve the main objective of each type of voiceover work, and

---

[39] "What Voice Actors Need to Know About 'Voice Matching.'"

3) To identify which type of voiceover work appeals to you most, initially.

This is the research phase of your plan to become a voiceover actor.

I am old school. I recommend getting a multi-subject binder for your research. Each type of voiceover work should have its own tab in the binder. If you are not old school like me, you can keep an online journal. The point is to have an organized place where you can keep notes on what you are learning as you train your ear.

With journal in hand, or online, your next step is to close your eyes and listen. Ask yourself a series of questions. Write the answers down for each example of voiceover:

- *How does it make you feel—one-word emotion?*

- *If the person were a character, how would you describe them?*

- *What is the talent doing technically to make you imagine where they are, who they are, and what they want you to do?*

I have already suggested other questions for specific types of voiceover work. The questions above are provided to initiate additional insight.

There are seemingly endless resources on the internet and elsewhere to take your ear on a listening tour of the world of voiceover recording and acting. I have collected a sample of some of the best examples of the work.

Examples of Voiceover Work

Below is a collection of resources to train your ear. Please take this step seriously and devote the time necessary.

Most importantly, listen to your voice within—does the work call to you? Does it make you eager to get started? Do you feel bored? Do you feel overwhelmed? Does it all feel silly?

Are you finding it difficult to get around to doing the research? Is your journal empty? The answers to all these questions are important.

You might discover that voiceover is not your passion after all. That is a win too. The sooner you know that voiceover is not for you, the sooner you can get on with discovering what is and get started on that.

Now it's time to begin your listening and learning tour of the voiceover world.

Voices.com and Bunnystudio.com[40] have examples of most types of voiceover work on their sites. These sites can be your one-stop shop for research. I have also provided some additional resources organized by the type of voiceover work.

Commercial Market

The most common resource for listening to and learning about top commercial voiceover work is iSpot.tv. The site contains a variety of the best television ads for products, services, and entertainment. The ads often combine live actors and voiceover.

Watching and listening to ads on this site will give you a good idea of the best of the best—and it is fun! The Voiceover.com site and its platform allows voiceover artists to promote their service. You will be able to listen to a variety of voiceover styles and gain insight into marketing techniques for voice actors. You will be listening to the demo reels, which will become important later. You will also see how different styles of voiceover are described. These descriptions, as you will come to understand, are not always precise or without some unfortunate baggage.[41] However, you will get a good idea of the field as it is now, how it describes itself, and where you might fit.

Animation and Gaming

A great place to start research on animation voiceover is to start with your favorite animated TV programs.[42] Linda Lamontagne, a noted and successful casting director for animation projects, recommends that you close your eyes while "watching" and listen for the tempo, rhythm, and projection in the performances of the actors.[43] For animation[44] and gaming voiceover work, you should listen for how well the voice actor creates a sense of character.[45] You should ask: How well

---

[40] See "Some Voice Over Film Examples for Your Entertainment - Bunny Studio."

[41] "VoiceOverXtra: \'I Am Not A Black Voice Actor. I Am Not An African-American Voice Actor. I Am A Voice Actor \'- Kabir Singh."

[42] Children's animated movies and TV: Moana; Frozen; Sponge Bob Square Pants; Toy Story Series; The Lion King; Princess Frog; The Incredibles; Arthur, The Magic School Bus; Clifford. Adult animation: Family Guy; Bob's Burger; BoJack Horseman. See also: "Best PBS Cartoons | List of Animated Kids Shows on PBS."

[43] See WachMojo.com https://youtu.be/0MLqW5i_eH8. See also their merciless list of the worst 10 voiceover video game performances. But it is instructive—see if you can distinguish the qualities that land performances on each list. https://watchmojo.com/video/id/24375#brid_cp_myDiv

[44] "Fan of 'The Simpsons'? Audition for These Animated Projects."

[45] You can explore more about what it takes to become a voiceover actor for gaming here: "Breaking into the World of Video Game Voiceover" and at "How to Be a Video Game Voiceover Artist." More on what it's like to be a video game voice talent can be found at "What It's Like to Work on Video Games, According to 'Mass Effect' VO Actor Jennifer Hale."

does the character you hear match the character on the screen? What techniques is the voice talent using? Is the character vocalization consistent throughout?

Examples of animation voiceover can be found at GravyfortheBrain.com and Voices.com. Examples of gaming voiceover can be found here on GravyfortheBrain.com.[46] WatchMojo.com has compiled a top ten list of best performances in gaming.[47] For an excellent discussion of what it takes to prepare for voiceover in animation, watch this excellent video by expert voiceover trainers Joan Baker and Rudy Gaskins.[48] I have also included a list of animation projects in this Guide that you can use for your research as well.

Explainers

You have probably already listened to voiceover in many explainer videos. When you watch videos for on-boarding at work, new software and devices, or services for your home or business, you are watching explainers. You probably did not pay much attention to the voice or notice what the voice actor was doing specifically to hold your attention and emphasize important information.

The Digital Brew website contains some terrific examples of explainer videos, as well as a helpful explanation of their process for developing them. This will provide good insight for future reference. More examples of explainers can be found at VideoExplainers.com. You can also find examples on Voicecrafters.com.

Corporate Narration

I consider corporate narration to be a subset of explainers. Much of your research about explainers will apply here as well. The Voices.com explainer video page has a good collection of corporate explainer videos. They also describe the qualities in voiceover work that are most important to corporate clients. According to Voices.com, corporate clients are looking for believable, friendly, conversational, authentic, and articulate performances. Voiceover actor Anne Ganguzza[49] has created a demo showcasing her corporate narration skills. Marc Scott's[50] demo provides another example of corporate work. You will also see how both Anne Ganguzza and Marc Scott promote themselves on their websites and on YouTube.

---

[46] You can also find a discussion of what it takes to get into anime voiceover work as well. "Anime Voice Over Jobs - Find How To Get Into Anime Voice Over."

[47] WatchMojo.com

[48] https://youtu.be/qwptXx_2Fq4. See also https://www.sovas.org/

[49] anneganguzza.com

[50] https://www.marcscottvoiceover.com/

As you continue your listening tour, make note of when and whether the voiceover trigger annoys you or makes you feel impatient. What is causing that response? Is it the pace? Is the voice actor speaking so quickly that it's difficult to grasp and process information? Are they speaking so slowly that you can anticipate each word? Hearing and understanding what is not working is as important as listening to exemplary work.

Audiobooks

You can find samples of audiobook performances on Gravyforthebrain.com, along with insights on how to get work in the audiobook field.[51] Amazon's Audible has compiled a list of the Best of the Best, Must-Listen Performances.[52] BookloverBookReviews.com offers "27 Best Audiobooks of the Decade, Narrators Worth Listening To." You will need a separate strategy for using this resource because there is just so much.

I would suggest that you listen to the samples and decide which type of book appeals to you. Then browse the recommendations in the genre or type of books you have chosen. Are you a fan of science fiction? Romance? Mystery? History? Select a book and listen from beginning to end.

Listen with your journal nearby. Note how the narrator makes you feel, how well the text comes to life, and what techniques the narrator uses.

Promos,[53] Radio/Podcast ID

VoiceCrafters.com has examples of promos as well as more information about making promotional voiceover videos. You can also find additional examples to listen to at Propodcastsolutions.com.

Looping/ADR Dubbing, Voice Matching

If you observe and listen to scenes in a television show or film that take place within a restaurant, stadium, bus or train station, or other public place, you are likely listening to voiceover talent working their craft. The unremarkable nature of the scene gives you a sense of the craft involved. The goal is realistically voiced conversation or sound. Voice actors working in ADR must use

---

[51] "Audiobooks Voice Over Jobs - Find Out All About Audiobook Narration."

[52] "Audiobooks Featuring Must-Listen Performances | Audible.Com." See also "The Best Black Audiobook Narrators to Listen To Right Now | Audible.Com."

[53] For additional background information on promo voiceover work see: "Everything You Need to Know About Promo Voiceover Work."

their improv skills and informed sense of their surroundings.[54] Here is a must-watch, fun video on ADR.[55]

For more information on ADR from the perspective of the filmmaker, you can watch the very helpful video called "What's ADR in Film and Why Is It Important?"[56]

Gadget/Product VO

Examples of voiceover for gadgets and products can literally be found at your fingertips: on your phone, on your desktop, or on your computer. When Siri[57] answers your questions, you are literally talking to a voice actor at work. Alexa, on the other hand, was originally not based on the work of a voice actor.[58] You may have talking scales in your kitchen or bathroom. Your children likely have talking animals and robots, pens, and books.[59]

Movie Trailers

Voices.com has many examples of voiceover work for movie trailers for your research and listening enjoyment.[60] They also have created an in-depth report on creating movie trailers that contains valuable additional information.[61] Movie trailers share much in common with promos and other advertising. When listening to the examples here, concentrate on the performance that engages you, creates a lasting impression, and motivates you to see the film.

IVR Systems Phone Casting/Store Casting

Examples of IVR systems phone casting and store casting can be found on the Gravyforthebrain.com website. David Lawrence XVII has produced an interesting video that, among other things, discusses specific techniques that he uses for effective IVR voiceover. He

---

[54] "ADR Voice Over Jobs - Find Out All About How To Get ADR Work."; "What's ADR in Film and Why Is It Important?"; "Looping and ADR - Bonnie Gillespie."; "What Voice Actors Should Know About Looping, ADR + Walla."; "What Voice Actors Need to Know About 'Voice Matching.'"

[55] https://youtu.be/mlx6VA98bQM

[56] https://youtu.be/7W46DjoFlGE

[57] Susan Bennet is the Voice of Siri. "Susan Bennett - Wikipedia."

[58] "Who Is the Voice of Alexa?" Now, however you can purchase the option of hearing Samuel L. Jackson's voice on Alexa. See "How to Talk to Samuel L. Jackson Using Alexa | Digital Trends."

[59] "Talking Pen Point Reading Pen For Educational Kids And Students - Buy Electronic Talking Pen, Educational English Book With Talking Pen, Kids Fancy Story Pens Product on Alibaba.Com." See also "Talking Products | LS&S, LLC."

[60] "Movie Trailer Voices - Best Voice Overs [Audio] | Voices.Com."

[61] "Movie Trailer Mastery | Complete Voiceover."

uses "pattern interruption," which is a way of using your voice to highlight important information.[62]

Chapter Summary/Key Takeaways

A warning and caveat—it will be easy to get lost in the forest of examples provided here. Your careful research plan is at risk of devolving into aimless wandering through websites. I know because I already did that for you. My recommendation is that you focus on one type of voiceover that interests you initially. If you need more information to decide, be disciplined about listening to only one example of each type. Then narrow your deeper research and the questions to a handful of examples in your chosen voiceover field. Use those examples for your journal.

Here is a summary of all the places where you can listen to examples of voiceover to sharpen your ear:

Source/Website	Voiceover Genre
Bookloversreview.com	• Audiobooks
Bunnystudio.com	• Advertising • Audiobooks • Characters • Educational • Live announcement • Movie trailers • Phone systems • Presentations • Product videos • Radio/TV tags
Digitalbrew.com	• Explainers
Hubspot.com	• Explainers
Gravyforthebrain.com	• Animation

---

[62] See: "Pattern Interruption And The Musicality Of Voice Over - Vo2gogo.Com" and https://youtu.be/OBZBtqF64JA

	• Audiobook • IVR Phone System Casting
iSpottv.com	• Commercial
Podcast.com	• Podcast promotional
Videoexplainers.com	• Explainers
Voicecrafters.com	• Explainer videos
Voiceover.com	• Commercial
Voices.com	• Animation • Business • Educational • Internet Video • Video Games

Here is a list of examples of animated TV and films. Note that many of the examples listed as designed for adults were designed to appeal to adults and children.[63]

Children	Adults
Arthur	BoJack Horseman
Clifford	Family Guy
Frozen	Bob's Burgers
Moana	Animal Farm
Mulan	Mary & Max
Rugrats	Loving Vincent

---

[63] Note that I am not making any recommendations about the suitability of any of the TV programs or films for children. This is simply your research database.

SpongeBob Square Pants	Lord of the Rings
The Incredibles	Howl's Moving Castle
The Lion King	How to Train Your Dragon 2
The Magic School Bus	Fantastic Mr. Fox
The Princess Frog	Our Friend, Martin
Toy Story Series	Inside Out

After your listening tour, you should have a comprehensive overview and understanding of the voiceover business. This insight should include direct experience with high quality work in one or more areas of interest to you.

You have notes on the voiceover work. You should have decided on one or two types of voiceover work that you are considering pursuing.

It is time now to examine the next tool in your starter-kit: your *voice.*

Chapter Three

Identify Your Tools: Your Voice

*The violinist in the story at the beginning of Chapter Two used a $3.5 million Stradivarius violin. The value of **your** instrument cannot be overstated.*

If you have trained as an actor, you are probably accustomed to thinking about your body and your voice as your instrument. This idea is no different for voiceover work. Being successful as a voiceover actor is more than being fortunate enough to have "a good voice."

You have listened to some of the best examples of voiceover work. Now it is time to focus on the technical aspects of using the voice. You have heard voiceover talent use pitch, tone, and rhythm to create the desired feeling or relationship to the copy being performed. It is time to learn more about the specific choices the voice actors made and why.

By definition, a voiceover actor is not seen. The usual tools available to convey emotion, intent, and objective are not available to the voice actor. Even for animation or a motion capture performance, the actor is hidden by the features and movement of the animated character or the animated version of themselves. While the actor's physicality and movements may influence the finished animation, the actor's full physical instrument is not accessible to tell the story and drive the plot.

Physicality and embodiment of a character can help voice talent shape their voice to portray a character. However, specific voice techniques and skills are required to deliver the performance.

Pitch, Rhythm, and Pace
Pitch is the sound of the voice heard moving along a scale from high to low in the same way a musical scale is played on an instrument.[64] A mastery and understanding of how pitch is used to

---

[64] See "Pitch: Public Speaking/Speech Communication."

convey thoughts, emotion, and character is an essential item in the voice actor's toolkit. It is often helpful for voiceover actors to listen to and think about the way they use pitch in everyday life to learn how to convey a clear objective.[65]

For example, without thinking, you likely end a question with the pitch of your voice going up.

*Are you going to the **library**?*

Here, you communicate openness to the answer or uncertainty.

That same sentence can convey a different meaning and situation if the pitch is changed in the sentence:

*Are you going to the **library**?*

Anger, impatience, even an order might be conveyed by simply making the pitch go down at the end of the sentence.

***Are** you going to the library?*

Change the placement of the elevated pitch in the sentence, and the same sentence become a challenge or accusatory.

---

[65] "Pitch: Public Speaking/Speech Communication."

At some level, these observations may seem obvious and basic, particularly for trained actors. However, now we must approach the familiar with clinical accuracy to use pitch with the intent, precision, and consistency necessary for voiceover work.

Understanding pitch will be important later to your approach to preparing and reading copy. Dancers use body awareness and muscle memory in the studio to construct a dance. As a voice actor, you must build a mental catalogue of tone, pitch, and muscle memory to construct a truthful performance.

The dancer is attentive to even the smallest muscle being used and the spatial alignment of the body. After much practice, the optimum alignment of the dancer's body and the precise contraction of the muscles are committed to memory. Similarly, the voiceover actor must practice and create muscle memory of those precise times when their voice most clearly and effectively conveyed the intended message. Like dance, it is a matter of recognizing when a technique is done correctly and repeating it until correct technique becomes automatic. It is a matter of replicating even minute adjustments in the body intentionally and in the proper sequence.

Voiceover artists often mark their copy to reflect changes in pitch and other direction for the performance. Afterward, they read the copy, hitting the benchmarks on the page. The voice actor follows the markings on a script much like a singer reads a score. As any trained singer will tell you, matching the voice to notes on a page is not easy or automatic. It takes practice to develop and perfect the skill. The same is true for the voiceover actor who must connect mind and body to bring words on a page to life.

Rhythm

American voice actor Fred Tatasciore[66] discusses rhythm, distinguishing it from tempo:

> Rhythm is the timing of sounds and silences that occur over time. Pacing, pauses, breath, the emphasis of key words, diction, and intonation comprise the rhythm of each voice acting performance. Whereas *tempo* is the overall speed of the performance, *rhythm* is the variations in speed.

---

[66] WonderCon, active 1982–present, "Fred Tatasciore - Wikipedia."

For Tatasciore and other voiceover professionals and instructors, observing and understanding the natural rhythm of your speech in different circumstances is the key to producing a natural voiceover performance. Some[67] recommend that you observe yourself when speaking in a variety of situations: When you tell a story about yourself or when you explain a complicated concept, when does your voice speed up? When does it slow down? When you prepare the copy, can you use that insight in your analysis? For example, imagine that you are telling your best friend a secret when you read the script for a commercial about a new dessert. How would the rhythm of your speech be affected?

Peter Drew[68] recommends reading your copy and grouping the words in "thought groups" to identify natural places where the idea changes. These are places where you would introduce natural pauses and changes in the speed of speech, all of which will make the copy sound more natural.

Leslie Bailey of Voiceovergurus.com recommends an additional technique to begin to obtain a natural sounding voiceover performance—listen to yourself and others in conversation. Where does your voice naturally speed up, slow down, get louder or get softer, for that matter?[69]

An appreciation and understanding of how to use rhythm is critical to creating a natural and therefore marketable performance.

Voice Quality, Diction, and Control

Voice quality is the actual sound of the voice. It is the thing that makes your voice unique. Voice quality has also been described as the voice timbre. Voice timbre means the quality of your voice, using complex overtones or sound waves. It can describe that unique "something" that gives color and personality to your voice. Voice timbre is what makes your voice uniquely recognizable.[70] It is the sound that is only produced by *your* instrument. If you study music, you know that no two pianos, violins, or even drums sound alike. The sound quality of the notes produced depends on

---

[67] "The Art of Voice-Over Cadences - Such A Voice."
[68] "Finding the Natural Rhythm in Voiceover Copy - Peter Drew Voiceovers."
[69] "Voice Over Gurus Blog | The Online VoiceOver Community."
[70] "Types of Vocal Timbre | Music To Your Home."

the design and shape of the instrument, the material used, and the precise breath, bow, or percussion mallet used to strike a note.

Your vocal instrument is much like other musical instruments. The production of your voice is a matter of physics.[71] The shape of your face, bone structure and density, soft tissues, and breath all influence the quality of the sound and voice produced.

It is therefore important that you gain an understanding of the physics of voice production to maximize your ability to enhance the quality of the voice and tell a compelling story.

Maximizing voice quality is not an artificial exercise. It is not an effort to feign gravitas—think caricature of an announcer. It is understanding how to maximize the instrument that you have been given to produce a sound that is as rich and full of you as possible.

<u>Diction</u>

Diction is the care and precision with which words are pronounced. Excellent diction ensures that the listener can understand what the voice actor is saying. Diction is often related to and connected to voice and sound production because the proper formation of consonants and vowels is related to the voice quality production.[72]

At TheVoiceRealm.com, Sam Parker quotes James Alburger, author of *The Art of Voice Acting*, describing diction "as the accent, inflection, intonation, and speaking style dependent on the choice of words."[73] Parker goes on to connect mastering of diction to the ability to use diction in the development of character.[74]

<u>Control</u>

Control in voiceover is the mastery of voice quality and diction. Mastery starts with an awareness of the voice and what it is doing. You then use these insights to marshal voice quality and diction

---

[71] See: *The Use and Training of the Human Voice, 3rd edition* (USA: McGraw-Hill, 1996). Arthur Lessac devised an entire system for maximizing the voice quality for actors and everyone. See also www.lessacinstitute.org.
[72] *The Use and Training of the Human Voice, 3rd edition* (USA: McGraw-Hill, 1996). Arthur Lessac devised an entire system for maximizing the voice quality for actors and everyone (throughout)
[73] "Diction in Voiceover – The Voice Realm."
[74] "Diction in Voiceover – The Voice Realm."

to tell a story and create a character. This will of necessity includes control of the breath and muscles necessary to produce the correct sound at the correct time.

Identify Your Tools: Train Your Voice

If you have a background in music, specifically singing, some of what follows will be familiar. You know the importance of training your voice to move through a range of pitches while maintaining consistent high-quality sound. In fact, my research for this Guide identified some excellent resources designed for singers. These resources that were designed for singers would likely also be beneficial for voice actors. Bottom line: the more you are aware of your voice and understand how you produce sound, and the more you have developed a responsive and flexible instrument, the more successful you will be in the voiceover business.[75]

If this seems overly complicated and dense at this point, do not get discouraged. While I have discussed each element in some detail, these elements are deployed together and organically as you learn, practice, and develop your voice.

Please also understand as you work with a vocal coach (which I will encourage you to do later) that they may take different approaches, emphasize different skills, or describe the actions differently. They may also use a variety of different techniques and drills to achieve the objective of cultivating a pleasant, natural speaking voice. The main goal here is to expose you to the general concepts and to emphasize the importance of training to develop your voice.

---

[75] This is just one example of the type of resources available if you want to focus on your voice as if you were a professional singer. "The Complete Guide to Improving Vocal Control - Ramsey Voice Studio."

<u>Musicality and sight reading</u>

Why discuss musicality and sight reading in a chapter about the voice? I highlight the topics here because sight reading and musicality are organically connected to the use of the voice. [76] Considering musicality is integral to preparing and reading copy,[77] all the work and awareness that has been discussed so far will prepare you for your mission critical task as a voiceover actor: *Reading copy. Reading a script.* With all of what has been discussed about voice, it might be easy to forget the most important and most difficult part of your job.[78]

For the dancer who spends hours in the studio preparing the body, perfecting each leap and pirouette, the goal is not the execution of a single step. The goal is the main event: the performance of the choreography of a dance.

Students of music who spend hours learning notes and practicing scales do so to perfect their ability to hit each note consistently and without fail. All of what has been discussed and your practice and training is to prepare you for the main event: reading the copy.

Preparation is the key to success in reading a script or copy. Preparation means taking the time to read the script several times. If you are preparing an audiobook, some suggest that you read the entire book first.[79] Reading the script in advance and knowing it gives you a roadmap of the narrative, allows you to identify unfamiliar words and names, and provides you with opportunities for research to learn the unfamiliar pronunciations.

The way in which you approach and analyze the script is an integral part of determining how you will use your voice and the concepts discussed in this chapter. Now that you are familiar with more of the basics, it is time to get practical.[80]

---

[76] If you want more information with tips and best practices for reading voiceover copy, you can start with the following. "Copy Reading. How Do Voice Actors Make the Narration Pop? Voice Acting Coach Rachel Alena Dishes…"; "Reading a Script | Voice Over Tips & Resources — The Voice Shop"; "Speed Reading - Why Voiceovers Need To Master This Art."

[77] "Pattern Interruption And The Musicality Of Voice Over - Vo2gogo.Com."

[78] While your ear is your most important tool and a well-trained voice is key—the task of reading a script or copy is the most important thing that a voice actor does.

[79] https://www.youtube.com/watch?v=7B4zPuY1-w0&list=RDCMUCbBRWl1PoeAjvuzGrVlbMhw&index=3-- This resource is frankly awesome.

[80] More information about the voice for voice actors, see: "The 4 Most Important Elements Of Your Voice."

<u>Find a voiceover coach: Get trained!</u>

When I first set out to write this Guide, I was neutral and even leaning against suggesting that a voiceover coach would be important to starting your career. I am generally skeptical of asking people to make large investments of money, especially when they are charting a new and untested course for themselves. This is even more my inclination in times when most people must be prudent and strategic with spending money.

However, my research has convinced me that finding a voice coach is an important step in determining whether the voiceover business is for you. If you decide that voiceover is a good fit for you, working with a coach is a great way to get started properly.[81]

The other factor is that you can take steps to mitigate what I view as the major risk: throwing good money after bad services.

It makes sense to find and work with a voiceover coach for the following reasons:

- ✓ Even with widely expanding opportunities in the voiceover business, it is still a highly competitive field. There are many people competing for jobs. You need to enter the market as close to the top of your game as you can. Working with a voiceover coach will shorten your learning curve. You will be able to create a marketable product that will get you selected for jobs. You will likely be prepared to enter the market sooner than if you train yourself alone.

- ✓ Voiceover coaches can provide you with a template, a checklist even, and a way of approaching the work that will avoid reinventing the wheel. Coaching will help ensure that you are always turning in your best, professional auditions. Even if you do not ultimately get the job, you will maximize your chances of leaving a professional impression while you continue to learn. You will learn and become familiar with the language and jargon of

---

the business more quickly. This will help you to communicate more effectively with professionals in the industry and help you better serve your clients.

✓ Developing your voice requires discipline and substantial practice. Working with a voiceover coach can provide the information and consistent framework necessary to systematically develop the voice. A coach can provide feedback and accountability to ensure that you put in the work.

✓ Voiceover coaches connect you to the broader voiceover community, which can lead to jobs, peer networks, and updates on the latest creative innovations and changes in the field. If you are working in a home studio, especially, working with a voiceover coach can help you overcome the isolation that can hinder a novice in the field. Being connected to others in the field and to a coach or mentor will increase your sense of purpose and well-being, which will result in better performances.

✓ Feedback is important to perfecting your skills and talent as a professional. While over time and with experience, your ability to listen to your performance and evaluate it will improve, there is no substitute for good, honest critique, provided it comes with concrete, actionable steps for improvement.

✓ While we all enjoy the stories about the novice with natural ability who lands a career-defining role right from the start, the likelihood of this happening is rare. Moreover, voiceover work is not hit or miss. It takes more than a beautiful voice. The reality is that successful voiceover actors make the appropriate investment of time and resources to learn the craft. Working with a voiceover coach provides you with a solid foundation to prepare you to be a top professional. The bottom line is this: even those with natural ability or previous acting experience should be trained by a voiceover professional to be at the top of your game. Natural ability and experience may influence the amount of training required. However, finding and working with a voiceover teacher or coach should be part of your plan.

The good news is that there are a lot of options for finding a terrific voiceover trainer or coach. The exponential growth of online and virtual learning opportunities makes it possible to work with the best voice trainer or coach for you, regardless of where you live. You have good choices among learning formats and fee structures as well.

<u>In-person, private training</u>

To the extent possible, my recommendation would be to start with a carefully selected voiceover training program or coach that works with you. You would normally start with a voiceover evaluation, which might be free or offered at a reasonably low to nominal cost. The evaluation would provide you and your coach with a baseline from which to develop your voice quality, technique, and acting ability.

The private session offered in-studio, if available, or virtually would provide you with the personal attention and feedback necessary to advance quickly. There is also no substitute for the accountability that comes from working one-on-one with a professional who knows you and expects the best from you. To make progress, you must devote time outside of your training sessions to advance. Having regular meetings with a coach provides an additional incentive to devote the necessary time to practice.

While you can work with a voice coach or trainer over a long period of time, if budget is an issue, you might consider a block of three to five sessions at a time. You can then work on your own to perfect what you learned with your coach. You can always book additional training sessions as your budget allows. Remember, developing as a voiceover actor is an ongoing process. There is no such thing as one and done. You should be engaged with a coach or trainer as much as you can. You need not always work with the same coach all the time. As your career develops, your training needs will change. As you specialize in one aspect of voiceover or another, you will want to identify coaches or trainers who have deep experience and expertise in that field. There are, for example, coaches that specialize in audiobooks and commercial copy.

As with everything, you must be an educated consumer. Backstage.com provides some good advice and recommendations for selecting a private voiceover coach or trainer. [82] Voiceacting.com[83] and Bunnystudio.com[84] provide important insights as well.

In addition to working with a voiceover coach individually, there are many online training opportunities. These opportunities include live group classes; workshops and group practice sessions; and video training sessions with opportunities for live, virtual practice and discussions. Many of these online opportunities offer specialized training in specific genres of voiceover, such as IDR or animation and gaming. These websites include access to free resources and information about the industry.

Many voiceover coaches/trainers and training website platforms provide consultation, evaluation, and set-up for your home studio. This service can be extremely helpful to a novice. It will be important to carefully evaluate the true value of what is being offered. This is especially true when services are offered as part of a package. The package that you are asked to purchase should be heavily weighted in favor of the training. Here again, a carefully selected voiceover coach can help you evaluate offers and provide you with sound advice for building your first home studio. Starting out, you should be aiming for the best of the basics.

<u>Pricing and fee structures</u>

Private one-on-one voiceover coaching can range in price from $125–$210 per hour. You can likely purchase classes individually; however, some voiceover trainers bundle them in groups. The bundle may include private sessions with demo consultation, direction, and production. Some coaches include consultation to you as well as assistance setting up your home studio in the package of services provided.

---

[82] "How to Find a Great Voiceover Coach." Backstage also has a roster of the best seven voiceover coaches based on feedback from knowledgeable and experienced people in the industry."7 Great Teachers to Kick-Start Your Voiceover Career." Noted voice actor Harlan Hogan has also compiled a list of voiceover coaches and trainers. See https://harlanhogan.com/coachList.php

[83] Voice Acting Academy, "Get Started in Voiceover."

[84] "Read This Before You Hire a Voice Over Coach - Bunny Studio." Marc Preston provides additional advice and "red flags" to watch for in deciding on your voiceover training. See "How to Choose a Reputable Voiceover Coach/Consultant." A number of voiceover websites, including Edge Studio.com; Voices.com; The Voiceover Gurus; Such AVoice.com; Global Voice Academy.

Voiceover Actor, Carrie Olsen provides excellent information. See https://carrieolsenvo.com/. She provides a free email training resource through her website.

Several websites offer access to online training including one-on-one training, video instruction, live group sessions, demo production, home studio set-up, and equipment purchase and discounts. Depending upon the services offered, the membership can range from nearly $50 per month to about $60 per month. Some websites offer services for a flat fee. These websites offer packages of training sessions, one or more produced demos, home studio consults, equipment purchase, set-up, and technical training. Several websites will allow you to split the payments into installments or make payments monthly.

Later in this Guide, we will discuss the importance of developing an initial voiceover budget. I want to emphasize that point now. If you are working from a solid budget that prioritizes your objectives, it will be much easier to make smart choices about your best options for training. When you start to look at the classes and see all that is available, or when you are enamored of a particular coach, you will want to spend all the money and take all the workshops. Having a set budget will provide a helpful check on this impulse.

<u>Practice</u>

One last point that goes hand in hand with training: practice. As much fun as voiceover work is and can be, it requires commitment, dedication, and personal discipline. The ideal situation is often to work from home, on your own time and schedule, and on projects that you select. However, a successful business in even that optimum setting requires discipline and focus. It is important to start building those muscles from the beginning. Disciplined focus on daily practice is a good place to start.

As I mentioned earlier, your voiceover coach or teacher will give you exercises with the expectation that you will practice the homework until it is mastered. Whether you are working with a voice coach now or not, your daily routine should include vocal exercises, reading aloud, and some daily exercise to keep your body—your instrument—fit.

You should be doing something every day for your craft. It does not have to take a lot of time. However, you should be doing something every day.[85] For example, as you prepare for the day

---

[85] It does not have to be the same thing every day. Some days you might focus on practicing diction; another day you might focus on developing breath control. Reading about developments in the field or watching a video on an aspect

and take a first look in the mirror, it might be the perfect time to exercise your face and try a tongue-twister. Read a favorite poem aloud before going to sleep. You do not have to do a dramatic reading; just practice reading the words slowly at different speeds. If you are working with a coach or have learned a set of vocal exercises,[86] add those to your routine. In thinking about the investment you are about to make, finding fifteen minutes a day for your craft will be invaluable.

Be good to yourself; if you miss a day, do not let it derail you. You can always begin again. Missing a day or more is part of the process; the key is to start again the moment you realize you are off track. If you are not feeling motivated to practice vocal exercises, you can read a paragraph of anything, preferably aloud. Pay attention if you find it difficult to get motivated to practice. Is this just too busy a time to make a big commitment to something new? Does the commitment required outweigh your initial interest in the work? There is no such thing as failure here. If you discover the process is not for you, that's good information and a success for your efforts. If you take the time to reflect, you may also discover that voiceover is your passion and that you must realign other aspects of your life with voiceover as the priority.

Chapter Summary/Key Takeaways

A voiceover actor must train and cultivate the voice. This includes perfecting tonal quality, diction, and the ability to use rhythm, pitch, and pace. Ideally, someone new to voiceover should begin by training with a reputable voiceover coach. You can work with an independent coach or find one through several well-known voiceover websites. You can also seek out group training opportunities and take advantage of free training resources that are available. Quality training is one of the most important financial investments that you can make for your career.

Finally, as you focus in on your voiceover career, now is the time to incorporate daily practice into your usual routines.

In the next chapter we will discuss "the read" in more detail and illuminate further the importance of seeking guidance and practice.

---

of voiceover work also qualifies as working on your craft. Maybe one day you only have time to practice one tongue twister in the mirror. Celebrate yourself and your commitment to being excellent at your craft.

[86] "(190) Lessac Structural Vowel Voice Lesson - YouTube." See also Arthur Lessac, *The Use and Training of the Human Voice: A Practical Approach to Speech and Voice Dynamics*, Third Edition (1997).

Chapter Four

Identify Your Tools: The Read

When I saw a photocopy of "15 Rules for a Dancer" on the bulletin board of a dance studio, I was so struck by the truth of the observations that I asked for a copy that I keep at home. The 15 rules apply to more than dancers. They apply to our subject matter here, too:

1. *Dance is hard. - No dancer ever became successful riding on their natural born talents only. Natural ability and talent will only get us so far. Dancers must work hard and persevere.*
2. *You won't always get what you want. - We don't always get the role we wanted, go on pointe when we want, get the job we want, hear the compliment we want, make the money we want. This teaches us humility and respect for the process, the art form, and the masters we have chosen to teach us.*

Voiceover work is art; it is a creative undertaking. Like any creative enterprise, we must honor it by educating ourselves and learn from those who came before us.

I have touched on the importance of "the read" and your ability to analyze copy. Discerning the context, place, objective, and qualities of the person you are portraying and the people around you are critical to telling a compelling story. Many of the techniques that you would use to prepare for film or stage work can be used to support voiceover work as well.

For audiobooks, animated films, and certain video games, traditional acting techniques can be easily adapted for voiceover work. You should read the book or script before you record it. This will allow you to learn important information about the story arc and character development.

The biggest challenge in voiceover for an actor is that you often are working alone. In other settings, you would have other actors to interact with and to build your performance. You would even have a director to give you feedback and home in on the meaning and objectives in the text. Even if you work in a studio setting with a client and a director, so much depends on *you*.

Your relationship to the text, and your ability to use your imagination with the text, become more important. The good news is that there are experienced voice actors and coaches who have cracked this code, so you do not have to start from scratch to figure out how to do it. Your time and energy can be better spent building your skills.

Identify Your Tools: Train Your Read

Unlike traditional acting where the goal is always to "get off book" as quickly as possible, in voiceover, the goal is literally to read the script. Voiceover copy, especially in the commercial market, may be more of a negotiated text than a work of art. This means that the client will expect you to read every word on the page accurately. The client likely will not be pleased with missed words, ad-libs, or paraphrases of the script.

It takes special skill to read every word on a page without sounding as if you are reading. In addition to mastering pace, pitch, and breath, you must literally practice reading words on a page while maintaining the proper proximity and alignment to a microphone.

Reading a script for voiceover can pose challenges for actors trained for film, television, and the stage. We pride ourselves on our ability to look away from the script to connect with the audience or camera. In my own experience, this approach is disastrous for voiceover. I lose my place in the text. My tendency to move my head, to look around for emphasis, creates inconsistent alignment with the microphone, which diminishes sound quality.

Reading a voiceover script requires you to retrain your eyes to follow along the script smoothly. Even when the role requires or allows you to move or gesture, you must keep a steady eye on the text. Therefore, practicing reading aloud as discussed earlier can be so important.

Get Practical: How to Do It

Find a voiceover trainer and coach who will teach you how to analyze and read voiceover copy. If you know now that you want to specialize in a particular aspect of voiceover work, look for a coach who specializes or has a focus on that aspect, because your approach to the copy will differ.

Look at sample voiceover copy that you can readily download from the web. Try reading it. Record yourself on your phone. Do you sound natural? Do you sound convincing, or do you sound like you are reading words on a page?

Make a note in your journal (remember your journal?) about what you heard in your voice that you liked. What did you hear that you did not like? What problems did you encounter when you first tried to read the copy out loud?

Once you have a voiceover coach, continue to find and download sample voiceover copy, and practice reading using the concepts and ideas that your coach has taught you. This should be your extra credit homework—because you want to be the best.

You can easily find sample voiceover copy online. Below are just a few places to get you started.

Website	Link	Comments
EdgeStudio.com	https://www.edgestudio.com/script-library/unregistered	Create a free account for access.
Voices.com	https://www.voices.com/blog/voice-over-sample-scripts/	Available from website without registration.
VoiceActorWebsite.com	https://www.voiceactorwebsites.com/free-voice-over-scripts/	Available from the website. Resources and free tools for voiceover talent.
Stagemilk.com	https://www.stagemilk.com/voice-over-scripts/	Voiceover script templates and short sample scripts.

Chapter Summary/Key Takeaways

In addition to helping you to develop your voice, a voiceover teacher or trainer is essential to helping you learn how to properly analyze and read copy professionally.

Take advantage of the wide variety of free sample voiceover scripts to see the range of copy and writing styles available. Most importantly, try reading sample scripts to get a sense of your strengths and challenges. Once you start working with a coach, use sample scripts to practice your technique.[87]

Chapter Five

Identify Your Tools: Your Set-Up

Dreams about the future are always filled with gadgets.

-- Neil deGrasse Tyson

You have done some really hard work. You have a good overview of the industry. You have a sense of what it takes to be successful in the industry. Now it is time to focus on the equipment you will need to build a solid, professional career as a voiceover actor. My overall advice is simple: work from a budget that prioritizes training and then purchase the best quality equipment you can afford within your budget to produce a quality professional sound.

The most expensive and elaborate equipment in the world will not compensate for a lack of technique and skill. Therefore, I insist that you prioritize training. You can find a comfortable spot in the middle where you have the training you need and the equipment you need to maximize your talent.

When it comes to equipment, you can always upgrade. You might consider developing an upgrade plan or schedule as your business develops. Your voice coach or trainer can also provide invaluable guidance about what brand and type of equipment to purchase. Be on the lookout for training and webinars for good advice, particularly those where the trainer does not also sell the equipment.

In this chapter, I will describe the major components of a home studio.

What follows is an outline of what you will need to set up your voiceover studio in your home.

You need the following set-up for your voiceover business:

> - A quiet environment for recording your voiceover auditions and projects
> - A microphone
>   - Headphones
>   - Compressor
> - A computer with
>   - Audio recording software

A Quiet Environment to Record

Critical to producing a professional voiceover project is having a quiet, distraction-free location where you can record. Your environment does not have to be soundproof. It just has to be consistently quiet. In addition, the space must be "dead," which means that sound does not bounce and reverberate off hard surfaces and does not echo. The space does not have to be big or even permanent.

The best and most expensive microphone and software alone will be for naught without the proper attention to your recording environment. You might be dreaming now about your state-of-the-art home-based voiceover studio. However, you do not have to start your voiceover business with a pricey investment.

Here are the basics: a quiet space that is as removed as possible from noise on the inside and outside. That means a spot as far as possible from outside noise, some distance from windows and doors that can let in traffic and street sounds. Also, you should be some distance away from the noise of refrigerators, dishwashers, air conditioners, and the laundry.

So, what are obvious possibilities? Some of the best options are a closet in your home. It does not have to be a large walk-in closet. You need only enough space to sit or stand and enough room to fit a music stand, mic, and mic stand or small table to hold your computer.

A note about computers: if you are using a laptop, be aware that the fans in laptops may emit a low buzzing sound. Desktop motors can be noisy as well. Consider how to position your laptop away from the microphone and consider the pick-up pattern for the microphone, which we will discuss later.

Keep in mind that the space need not be a permanent, dedicated space. You don't have to give up your closet entirely.[88] The space need not, and will likely not, be completely soundproof. The goal is to make the space as quiet as possible.

In addition to the space being quiet, the space needs to be "dead." Dead space is a space that does not allow sound to bounce around. If you want to get a sense of what dead space does not sound like, go into your bathroom, clap your hands or say a few words, and listen. You will hear the

---

[88] I have been amused to see photographs of lawmakers and celebrities recording podcasts from their closets at home—wedged in with coats, suits, and dresses around them. It is a smart idea because the clothes serve to deaden the sound and replace blankets and acoustic foam.

sound reverberating: that is not what you want, which is why you should not set up your voiceover studio in your bathroom.

To create dead space, you need materials to absorb the sound so that it does not bounce around. You can invest in acoustic foam which can be attached to walls using temporary mounting adhesive, or adhesive if you can permanently alter your space. You can find acoustic foam online that can be used to cover walls and ceilings in your home studio. You can also use blankets and comforters to cover walls. You can buy special blankets made for audio booths, but regular blankets and comforters can work just as well. In addition to covering the walls and ceiling, you should consider carpeting the space as well.

If you are creating a voiceover studio or booth in your closet, you may not need acoustic tiles or blankets if the closet is full of clothes. The clothes will deaden the sound. Add a floor covering and you are finished.

There are also smaller portable booths which are essentially acoustic-foam-lined boxes large enough to fit your microphone and your head. You can even find larger portable studios that can fit many budgets.

The bottom line is this: When it comes to the proper environment for voiceover recording, my advice is to start modestly and invest only as much as required to achieve a professional sound. I would recommend first repurposing a multi-use space. The key is to find the quietest location available to you and then to reduce the amount of sound reverberation around you. As the resources in the footnotes demonstrate, this can be done in the corner of a room skillfully, if not artfully, with pillows and blankets. If you have a closet that otherwise meets the requirement of being in a relatively quiet location, you can record there, and the only acoustic treatment you need might be the clothes already hanging in the closet.

If you are feeling more ambitious, you might clear the closet out and outfit it with blankets or with acoustic foam. You will need to add access to electricity if it is not already there. You can often use an extension cord safely as a workaround.

One other idea: when you purchase your microphone and USB adapter, and decide whether to buy a pre-amplifier, keep your environment in mind. The pre-amplifier can help with—not eliminate— some of the challenges of a less than optimum environment with the proper match of audio equipment.

<u>A Microphone</u>

You will need a microphone that will help you produce the best quality sound. Microphones have two main jobs: to pick up sound and transmit the sound so that it can be recorded.

There are three types of microphones:[89] condenser, dynamic, and ribbon. Condenser microphones pick up sound in an omnidirectional pattern and can have the capacity to change their pickup patterns. Dynamic microphones pick up sound in a cardioid pattern. Ribbon microphones pick up sound in the bidirectional pattern.

- Condenser--Omnidirectional

Omnidirectional microphones pick up sound from all directions.[90]

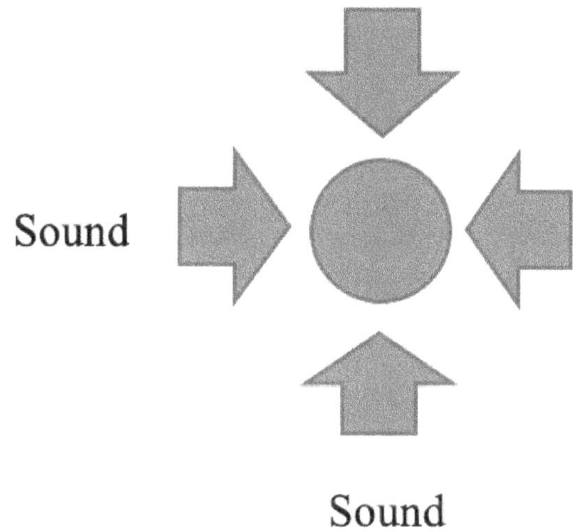

---

[89] "A Guide to Microphone Types and Placement | Home | Reverb News."
[90] "A Guide to Microphone Types and Placement | Home | Reverb News."

- Dynamic--Cardioid[91]

These microphones pick up sound in a heart-shaped pattern but not from the rear.

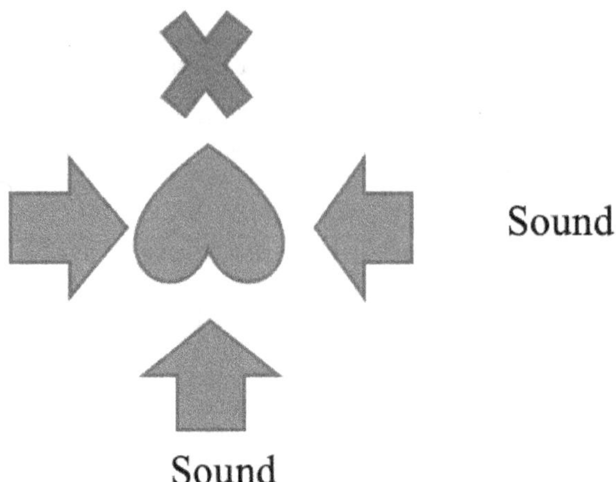

- Ribbon--Bidirectional[92]

These microphones pick up sound from the front and the back but not from either side of the microphone.

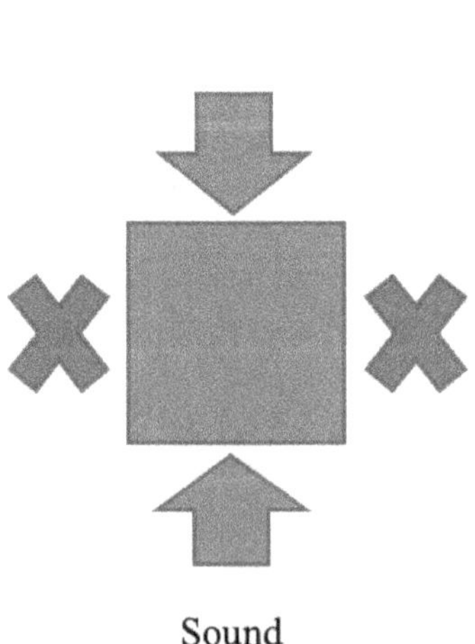

---

[91] "A Guide to Microphone Types and Placement | Home | Reverb News."
[92] "A Guide to Microphone Types and Placement | Home | Reverb News."

The best microphone for voiceover would be a condenser microphone, which can be switched to a bidirectional pick-up pattern to minimize background noise. In choosing your microphone, once again, guidance from your voiceover coach and trainer will be helpful for identifying which microphone will best capture and showcase your voice. As always, the touchstone for your decision should be your budget. The good news is that you can find a good quality microphone that will produce a professional voiceover product. I've included links to several websites that will give you an overview of types of microphones; they are available in the footnotes.[93]

You can start off with a USB microphone that plugs directly into your computer. But you may want to consider upgrading to a USB audio interface which converts the signal from higher performing microphones that would not connect directly to your computer. If you are in a location where noise is a problem or if you want to further improve your sound quality, you should consider adding a preamplifier[94] to your system as well.

Computer and Software Requirements

The good news is that you likely already have a computer that will run the software necessary to record your voiceover performances. And more good news: there are a number of free software programs that will serve you well as you build your experience and work portfolio. Below are several of the most popular voiceover programs and their technical requirements.

As you gain experience and make connections in the voiceover community, you will learn of other recommendations. Your voiceover coach may know of others. You will know when you are ready and it is time to invest in more expensive software. The same will be true about when to upgrade your computer set-up as well.

Audacity

Audacity is a free open-source software program. Any computer made after 2003 should be able to run the Audacity program. In addition to finding additional and more detailed technical requirements for Audacity, the Audacity Wiki provides a complete compatibility table with the most up-to-date information.

---

[93] "A Guide to Microphone Types and Placement | Home | Reverb News."
[94] "What Is a Preamplifier? Why Do We Need Them? | LedgerNote."

Audacity is easy to learn and use functionally. The Audacity website[95] provides useful resources including a manual with a list of tutorials ranging from "Your First Recording" to advanced editing techniques. YouTube videos can help get you started and provide you with confidence in using the program and gaining valuable experience with the platform.

GarageBand

GarageBand is a free software program designed for Mac computers. While GarageBand is best known as software for music recording, it has a significant following among voiceover performers.[96] The GarageBand website contains tutorials and resources that help you get started. There is not a GarageBand version for PCs but there is a workaround.[97]

The Wondershare Filmora has a rundown of the Top 10 Audio programs.[98]

Chapter Summary/Key Takeaways

The basics of a voiceover set-up are your recording environment, your microphone, and your computer and software. You should invest modestly when setting up your home studio and consider starting with space and materials on hand, because you can always upgrade.

The best microphone for voiceover would be a condenser microphone which would have a bidirectional pick-up pattern to minimize background noise. You will need a USB adapter and you should consider adding a preamplifier if your surroundings are noisy.

You can likely use your current home computer set-up if your computer is no more than three years old. As for software, start with free audio software. Audacity has a popular following and if you have a Mac, GarageBand is also popular.

---

[95] "Audacity Manual."
[96] See: "How To Use GarageBand on a Mac - Easy Tips & Pointers | Voices.Com."
[97] "GarageBand for Windows 10 PC - Download & Install [2020]."
[98] "Top 10 Audio Recording Software to Capture Your Voice Easily." See also: "The Best Audio Editing Software for 2020 | PCMag."

Chapter Six

Identify Your Tools: Marketing

There are hobbies and there are businesses. Neither is of more value than the other. You just need to be clear in which enterprise you are engaged and you will be fulfilled in your success. If it is a business you are engaged in, you must approach voiceover work with the rigor and determination of the most astute Fortune 500 CEO or successful small business entrepreneur.

At this point, we are probably getting a little ahead of ourselves to talk about marketing because you are just at the very beginning of your voiceover journey. First, you must train and set up your home studio. Soon, however, it will be time to look for your first job. You will want to start auditioning. What follows next is an overview of what it means to begin to get your name and voice out in the world and start getting work.

There are four major components to a voiceover marketing strategy: your voiceover demo tape; your professional website; networking; and whether and when it is time to seriously look for and sign with an agent.

The Demo Tape

In the earlier chapters of this Guide, when you trained your ear, you probably listened to voiceover demos.

The demo tape[99] is a professionally produced sample of your work which shows a potential client or employer what you can do. It is your calling card and your best tool for getting an audition, which leads to the opportunity to get hired. But what if you have not worked yet?

If you don't have sample work for your demo tape, use copy that you write yourself and record to showcase your style and range. There is a wealth of sample copy available on several websites to provide inspiration.[100] Do not, however, make the mistake of simply recording these scripts for

---

[99] See: "Voice Over Demo Scripts: Everything You Need to Know"; "Planning Your Voice-Over Demos | Voices.Com."

[100] "Voice Over Demo Scripts: Everything You Need to Know." See also: "Voice Over Sample Scripts | Edge Studio"; "How To Make A Voice-Over Demo"; "Free Voice Over Scripts - Read, Print & Practice Ready Voice Acting Scripts."

your demo. These sample scripts are best to use for practice, and to acquaint yourself with the style and unique aspects of various segments of the voiceover market. When you use sample scripts for your demo, you are likely recording copy that others have used. Moreover, the sample copy likely will not showcase your best features. If you are fortunate to have a voiceover coach, they might be willing to write and help you record copy designed especially for you.

If you are interested in working in more than one sector of the voiceover market, for example in commercial *and* animation, you should create a demo tape for each type of voiceover work.

The demo tape is not something you should produce yourself as an amateur, any more than you would show up to an interview in a suit that you had sewn yourself—unless you are a tailor. The field is competitive, so you must put your best foot forward. Investing in a professionally produced and directed voiceover demo is as important as investing in the right microphone for your home studio.

This is also when working with an experienced professional voice coach can give you a head start. The demo should be produced after you have had some training and mastered your technique. Your coach may be able to select and provide copy and may even be able to help produce the demo. My recommendation is to approach the two issues separately to avoid confusion and conflicts of interest—meaning focus initially on the training and then as the relationship develops and your technique improves, ask your coach for advice and help in producing the demo.

<u>Professional Website</u>

Now that you have your professionally rendered demo, what do you do with it? Well, of course you are going to want to get the demo in front of as many people as possible. You need a home base where people can come to find out more about you. The good news is that you can create a simple, professional website for free in a couple of hours. A basic voiceover website should feature your demo(s), and a resume or description of your work. If you do not yet have voiceover credits, you can highlight your acting credits and training. You also need to provide potential clients with a way of contacting you for auditions. Your website is where you can showcase your unique image with carefully chosen photographs and headshots or images.

You can build a simple free website on Weebly.com[101] which makes it relatively easy to create a simple website in a couple of hours. Wix.com[102] also offers the opportunity to create a free website.

<u>Casting Websites</u>

Several voiceover websites connect voiceover talent to potential clients and employers. The arrangements vary. Some post voiceover demos as part of a membership agreement. Some serve as a platform that connects and facilitates payment between voiceover talent and prospective clients.[103] Potential clients listen to demo reels on the platform and select the voiceover actors they want to audition.

You should get advice from your voice coach, others in the voiceover community, and online reviews to choose the site that provides the best rates and opportunity with the least hassle.

<u>The Agent</u>

A voiceover agent can help you get work in exchange for a percentage of the fee that you charge. Most agents will charge between 10% and 15%.[104] If you are a member of SAG-AFTRA, the most your agent can charge is 10%.[105] SAG-AFTRA members must work with SAG-AFTRA franchised agents.

When is it time to find an agent? Not a minute before you know you need an agent. Seriously, your chance of landing an agent increases once you have some training and experience under your belt, and a good professional demo.[106]

The agent will be looking to see how well your voice and brand[107] fit into the market they work in, and how easy and professional you are to work with based on your past work. In addition to booking your work, a good agent will help you focus on your goals and career objectives and give

---

[101] "Create a Website with Weebly's Powerful Website Builder." See: "Weebly Pricing - Compare Website Builder Plans and Pricing."

[102] "Wix Pricing Information | Upgrade to a Premium Plan | Wix.Com."

[103] "Search Voice Actors By Voice Over Category | Voices.Com." See: "How To Find And Hire A Voice Actor Online | Voice Over Website."

[104] "Getting a Voice Talent Agent | Voices.Com."

[105] See AFTRA Regulations Governing Agents Rule 12-C Regulations Of Members' Dealings With Agents As Amended July 1, 2002

[106] See: How To Get A Voiceover Agent with Gabrielle Nistico for an informative honest discussion of the question about when to seek out a voiceover agent. See: "How To Get a Voice Agent - Tips from a Top Voice Agent."

[107] Siegel, Cecelia, *Voiceover Achiever*.

you guidance about what steps you need to take to make yourself marketable. They may have suggestions about branding, updating your website, and creating a new demo reel tailored to the specific market for your talents.

I recommend seeking out an agent after you have put in some time being your own agent and doing your own business marketing. You will have a better sense of yourself, your voice, and your brand as the product. You will also gain a good sense of all the work that goes into marketing, which will give you better insight into the value and effectiveness of your agent when you do hire one.

While it is true that a good manager does not have to have done the job of the people being managed to be successful, there is no doubt that having done the job puts you in a strong position to evaluate the performance of the work being done. Further, once you have an agent, your marketing and outreach does not and should not end. Your agent should expand the contacts, networks, and connections available to you, which will yield increased opportunities for auditions and work. However, it is critically important that you continue to expand your network and connections as well, bringing those into your agent's orbit.

Remember, you will not be your agent's only client. You will only be the number one priority for you. No one will ever be as invested in your success as you. So you must never cede control of your destiny and career to others. If, however, your agent sees you working as hard as they are to get your name out there and bring new contacts into the office, I can almost guarantee that a good agent will see their role as maximizing your efforts. You will get priority attention over someone taking a more passive approach.

Marc Cashman,[108] writing for Backstage, provides some additional valuable insights—including questions to ask a prospective agent. Among his many great suggestions is that when looking for an agent, start by getting a list of franchised agents from your local SAG-AFTRA office. This is great advice. While SAG-AFTRA does not endorse or promote any one agent over another, the list does represent agents that are prepared to abide by a set of standards regarding fees and professional conduct.

The good news is that if you wait to seek out an agent until you have some experience and strong connections in the field, you will have access to ample suggestions and advice to help you find the

---

[108] "Finding + Landing a Voiceover Agent." See also: "Getting a Voice Talent Agent | Voices.Com."

right voiceover agent for you. Voiceacting101.com [109] provides a comprehensive and novel approach to seeking out voiceover work that is worth considering. The discussion includes a solid plan for finding an agent and links to lists of agents across the country. VO Agent Alliance is an alliance of independent voiceover agents that have made common ground to advance their view of what is in the best interest of the voiceover community.

<u>Voiceover Work is a Business</u>

If there is one point to drive home, it is that voiceover work is a business. If you do not approach it as such, you might have fun setting up your home studio, but you will not actually get much work.

The good news is that because it is a business, the general tools and approach to a business are available to you. There are many resources online to help you develop a business plan. Such A Voice makes a strong case about the importance of developing a plan.

Gravy for the Brain[110] has a phenomenal resource for building a business plan.

Key questions for developing a business plan:

- Goals and objectives
    - How much money do you want to make?
    - Who do you want as a client?
    - What is your timeline for achieving your goals?
- Focus
    - What segment of the voiceover business do you want to focus on?
    - What market is the best for you?
- Strategy
    - What is your plan for meeting your objectives?
    - What activities (tactics) will you engage in to meet your objectives?
- How will you measure your success? What benchmarks will let you know whether you are making progress?

---

[109] "Find Voice-Over Work & Voice Acting Jobs (Ultimate Guide)." Additional resources and links: "Getting an Agent – I Want To Be A Voice Actor!"; "Do I Need An Agent For Voice Over Work? | Voquent"; "Do You Need a Voiceover Agent? | The Voiceover Gurus"; See also: How to Get An Agent for Voice Acting. Some terrific insights here as well: Finding a Voiceover Agent - How To Be a Voice Actor.

[110] "Voice Over Business - How To Create A Thriving VO Business."

> ➢ <u>Global Voice Acting Academy.com</u> provides a rate guide with union and non-union rates to help you charge appropriate rates for your work—a terrific resource.[111]

> ➢ <u>Voiceoverview</u> is a business management tool that helps you track auditions, jobs and payment, and prospects and clients. The product also allows you to create a free webpage for marketing. Voiceoverview also allows you to create a free account for 30 days. After the free trial period, you can choose to pay a monthly or annual fee.[112]

<u>Chapter Summary/Key Takeaways</u>

Working in voiceover is a business. To be successful, you must use the tools that businesses use to be successful: you need a plan that sets clear goals, benchmarks, strategies, and tactics to achieve your goals. Your business plan must include a marketing strategy. You will need a professional demo tape, tailored to the specific clients and work you want to attract. You need a website so that clients can find you. You will need to develop a plan for networking and building connections that will get your name and work in front of potential clients.[113]

---

[111] "GVAA Rate Guide | Global Voice Acting Academy | Voice Over Coaching & Classes."

[112] Current fee is $9.99 per month or $96.00 annually as of October 2020.

[113] "Voiceoverview - Voice Over CRM and Voice Actor Business Management Tool." This is a great tool for tracking clients and prospects.

Final Thoughts

At the beginning of this Guide and at the beginning of this journey, you committed to study and practice to perfect your voice and your talent. You committed time to daily practice. The other side of this equation is that you will need to devote a similar amount of time to learning as much as you can about the business.

By now you might be feeling overwhelmed by all the information presented in the Guide. It probably seems as though it has been years since you were listening to commercials and thinking about ears and practicing funny exercises with your voice. Then we discussed microphones and you started thinking about building a home studio in your apartment. Now we are discussing teaching yourself an MBA course in marketing. It must feel as though you have fallen down a rabbit hole, leading to an endless number of other rabbit holes. It is time to take a beat, breathe, and get organized.

Before you go any further—it is time to stop and ask yourself whether a voiceover career is what you really want to do—given all that you now know it entails.

If the answer is *no*—it is just too much, and too much of what is required are things that I have no interest in doing—that is okay. This has been a success. My work here is done. My goal was to give you an overview of the field and what it will take to get you started on the way to being a success.

If the answer is *yes,* or even just maybe—you may still be overwhelmed but something about all of this is calling you—great! The next step is to begin to organize and prioritize the information here to provide actionable, manageable steps.

My recommendation is that you focus the bulk of your initial energy on determining the quality of and perfecting your voiceover talent. With advice from your voiceover coach and some of the resources here, build a simple home studio set-up where you can practice and submit a few auditions as they arise. Think about it: lawyers don't attempt to try cases and doctors do not try to treat patients before they have substantial training under their belts from school. While law and medical students might participate in clinical experience, these opportunities come after significant training and skills-building has taken place. These careers are viewed as lifelong occupations where it makes sense to take the time to invest in building expertise that will be enhanced over a long period of time.

If you think of building your voiceover career in this way, it can take some of the anxiety and pressure off. The amount of information and opportunities to engage with a range of voiceover professionals has exploded. So, you will need to be thoughtful and judicious in using your time.

In the first stage of your journey, you will want to focus on your education and training. Make your greatest time and resource investment there. After some training, when you have developed an overall understanding of the work and have a personal plan for enhancing your strengths, you should consider your equivalent of a clinical program. This would be the time to focus on building your simple home studio—investing in equipment that can grow with you. You might submit for auditions and, with the guidance of your voiceover coach, create your first demo tape.

Later, perhaps you can begin to focus your attention on addressing the business side. You might reduce the number of coaching sessions and begin to use the time to delve more deeply into the resources provided here on building your business and to do your own research.

In the context of this chapter, when you are ready, I encourage you to come back to it and dig deeper into the resources. For now, it is enough just to know that the resources are here when you are ready. Because I know that you can focus on the task at hand and read a little ahead in the syllabus, I am providing the chart below with one or two resources you can peruse as you focus your initial energies on your voice training.

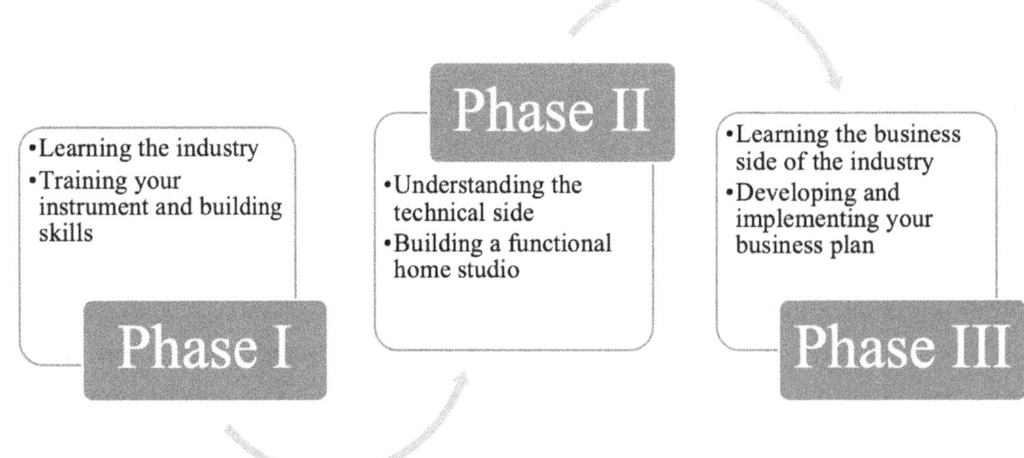

Depending on the time and resources you have available, you can determine how long you want to devote to each stage and the process overall. It could take months or several years. The trick is to develop a sense of competence that lets you know internally (and with appropriate feedback) when you are ready to move to the next phase. Your sense of satisfaction at your achievements should come not from the speed with which you move through the process, but from the fact that you are moving through the process on the schedule that *you have envisioned.*

What Is Not Covered in This Guide

There are topics that are important to your voiceover career that are not included in this Guide. They should nevertheless receive some attention. Fortunately, the timing will be right to focus on them as you begin to hit your confident stride in Phase III.

Taxes. You will have to pay them. You will want to consult an accountant or lawyer on the tax implications of your voiceover business.

- Self-employment, estimated taxes, business taxes—federal and local business licenses and taxes.
- What, if any, expenses related to your voiceover business might be deductible?

Client and business management. You will need to do it.

- What tactics and strategies should you use on an ongoing basis to cultivate and maintain relationships with existing clients and grow your share of business with them?
- How do you expand your client base and reach new markets?
- How do you stay on top of billing and invoicing? When do you need to get outside help with your accounting and administrative needs?

Summary

We have just taken a loud, wet splash in the voiceover pool and you have decided that you would like to learn to swim. Let us review what it will take from you to get into your best racing form for the challenge:

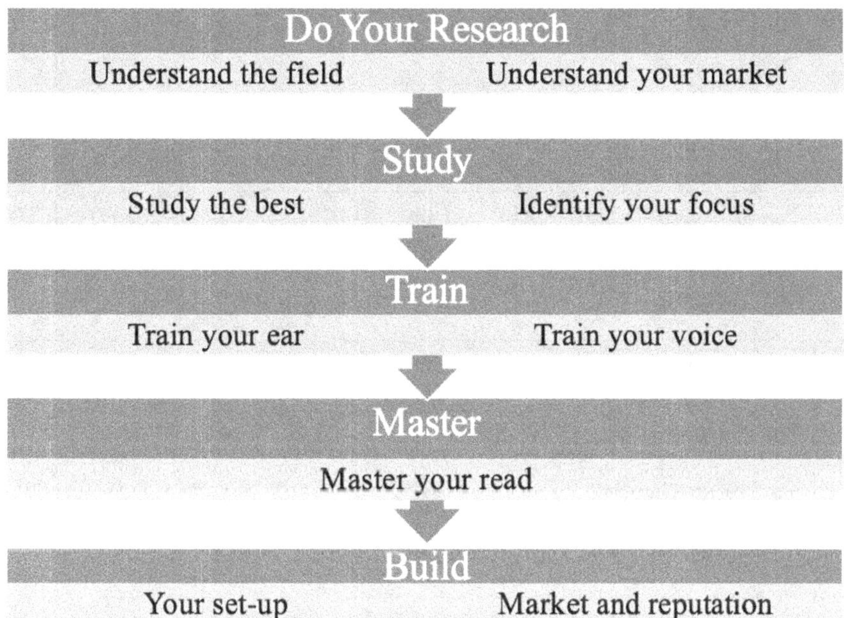

Glossary [114]

AAC	A type of audio file format. The default format for Apple Music/iTunes, iPod.
Account	An advertising client or customer.
Ad-lib	Improvised addition to a written script.
ADC	Analog to Digital Converter. This device records sounds and the voice and converts them to a numerical language that can be understood and manipulated by computers.
Adjustment	Feedback on a performance given by a director or a client to change the actor's approach to, and performance of, the script. Often called direction.
ADR	Automatic Dialogue Replacement. Recording dialogue after the video has been shot. Dubbing in multiple languages or recording audio for crowd scenes.
Agent	A person who represents an actor or voiceover talent, arranges for auditions, and books employment. This person takes a percentage of the fee paid to the actor as compensation for connecting the talent to the opportunity.
Air	The time assigned for a commercial or advertisement to run.
Aircheck	A recording of a broadcast radio program.
Algorithm	A process, procedure, or formula that will produce a desired result.

---

[114] This Glossary, including a selection of voiceover terms, is based on the voiceover vocabulary compiled by "That's Voiceover!" founders and Backstage experts Joan Baker and Rudy Gaskins. "Glossary of Voiceover Terms All Actors Should Know." This Glossary and a selection of terms is also based on the Glossary compiled by the Global Voice Academy. "Glossary of Voice Acting Terms | Global Voice Acting Academy | Voice Over Coaching & Classes." Finally this Glossary and a selection of terms is based on the Glossary compiled in the Audacity Development Manual "Glossary - Audacity Manual." I have not included all of the terms listed in these glossaries and, in particular, have excluded some of the very technical terms that you are not likely to encounter early in your voiceover career. Please consult the cited Glossaries for more detailed information and additional terminology not listed here. See also "38 Voiceover Terms All Voice Actors Should Know."

Ambiance	Sound effects or background sound accompanying voiceover which places the dialogue or voice in a specific place such as a train station.
Amplitude	The level or loudness of a sound.
Analog	The old way that sound used to be recorded on tape.
Animatic	An early version of a commercial ad with a story board with music and voiceover.
ANNC	Abbreviation for announcer used in a script to indicate what the voiceover talent will be reading.
Announcement	Commercial or advertisement.
Announcer	Voiceover talent.
Announcery	A style of voiceover associated with old style radio, often loud, over-the-top dramatic, and over-enunciated.
Arc	The emotional stages or trajectory of a storyline at the beginning, middle, and end.
Articulation	Clear pronunciation or enunciation.
Artifact	Unwanted sound that results from editing another sound.
ASIO	Audio Stream Input/Output audio digital protocol for Windows.
Audacity Project Format	The format that Audacity uses to store its files.
Audio	Transmission and/or reproduction of sound.
Audiobook	Recording of a book being read aloud.
Audition	A trial performance of a voiceover or acting job used to determine whether a particular actor or voiceover talent is a good fit for a role.
Availability	The time periods during which an actor is free to record a session.
Back bed	The part of a commercial jingle reserved for location and important information such as legal disclosures.
Background	Sounds or noise placed behind the voiceover to simulate a real place and location—for example, traffic sounds.
Balls	A deep sound.

Bandwidth	BPS - Most common measurement for the rate at which information is transmitted—the number of bits or units that can be transmitted between two devices in a second.
Beat	A thought that causes the speaker to pause in speaking a line.
Bed	The music or sound effects (SFX) that you hear under the voiceover.
Billboard	To emphasize a particular word in a script, for example the name of a pro.
Bit	A unit or measure of data.
Bit rates	The number of units of data processed over time.
Bleed	Noise from headphones or other background noise being picked up by the microphone.
Board	The audio console which an audio engineer operates.
Booking	A commitment by a client or employer to hire an actor or voiceover talent.
Boom	Overhead microphone stand.
Booth	An enclosed sound-treated space where voiceover recordings are created.
Branching	Recording different versions of parts of a sentence to provide the option for different outcomes—used in video games and telephone systems.
Branding	Marketing, strategy advertising signature.
Break up	When vocal sound is distorted due to equipment malfunction or issues with signal interference.
Broadcast or Broadcasting	Transmission of audio and video signal.
Bump	To remove someone from the cast list, or add additional time to a studio session.
Butt-cut	When video files are placed closely together.
Button	A single improvised word or phrase that makes a commercial spot memorable or nails the point but does not add new information.
Buy	The amount spent to purchase advertising time called a spot, the audio- or video-take that the client approves.

Buy-out	Onetime fee paid to voiceover artist.
Byte	A unit of measurement for information storage.
Cadence	Pace, rhythm, timing, and placement of breaks between words.
Call letters	The letters assigned to radio stations by the FCC.
Call time	The time scheduled for an actor to arrive for an audition or performance.
Call-back	A second opportunity to audition.
Cans	Headphones.
Castings	Process for selecting actors and voiceover talent usually involving in-person or self-taped submissions.
Cattle call	An audition where actors are asked to tryout in large groups.
CD-ROM	Compact disc read only memory.
Character	The role or person that the actor is hired to play.
Class A	National commercial network use.
Cold read	When actors or voiceover talents are given a script to perform, with little or no opportunity to prepare.
Cold reading	An audition where the actor is required to perform a script without having prepared.
Color	Approach to the way in which words are spoken to given them added meaning and subtle nuance.
Commercial	A pre-recorded advertisement for a product or point of view, issue, or candidate.
Compressed and Audio format	A format that reduces the space necessary to store audio files.
Compression	A process that evens out the overall volume level of an audio recording, so that the volume is consistent throughout.
Conflict	Performing in a second commercial for the same type of product.
Console	Equipment that the audio engineer uses to monitor, edit, and mix an audio recording.

Control room	The place where the audio engineer monitors, edits, and mixes audio recordings.
Conversational	A natural, everyday way of speaking, using normal tones and without dramatic emphasis.
Copy	The script. The text that is read aloud by the voiceover talent or actor.
Copy points	The aspects in the script or copy about the product that the client or employer wants the voiceover talent to emphasize.
Corporate presentation	A performance or demonstration that is meant to be shown internally at a company and not for distribution to the public.
Creative Director	The person responsible for the advertising work and all the people who create the advertising, writers, graphics, and video and talent.
Cross talk	When audio spoken by one voiceover actor is picked up by another voiceover actor's microphone.
Cue	A signal given to the actor to begin the performance.
Cue up	Matching the voiceover with visuals on the screen.
Custom demo	A sample audio recording of a specific script with various actors that helps the client choose the voice talent best suited for the job.
Cut	A segment of a voiceover recording.
Cut and paste	Combining specific segments of recorded audio into a single audio project.
Cutting through	When a voice comes through over music or background sounds.
DAC	Digital to analog conversion.
DAT	High quality digital audiotape.
dB	Abbreviation for decibels.
Dead air	A pause in a voiceover recording—extended unscripted silence.
Decibel	A unit for measuring the intensity of sound.
Demo	A voiceover talent's sample performance used to get auditions.
Demographics	The target audience for voiceover commercial or spot.

Dialogue	Script with conversation between two people.
Digital recording	A process for converting audio to numerical symbols that can be stored on the computer.
Director	The person who guides a voiceover in the performance.
Distortion	When the sound does not come across clearly in audio recording.
Donut	A voiceover commercial or spot that features an additional voice.
Double	Commercial that has more than one voiceover character.
Drive time	The time during the day when the most people are listening to the radio.
Dropoff	Weak ending at the end of a word or a phrase.
Dropout	Silence within a word or phrase in a recording.
Dry mouth	A condition when there is insufficient saliva in the mouth.
Dry read	The reading of copy by a single voiceover talent, where there is no music or background noise underneath the voiceover.
Dub	A copy of an audio track.
Dubbing	Transferring a copy of an audio recording onto another medium.
Dynamic range	The difference between the loudest and the quietest part of an audio recording.
Earphones	Device worn during a recording to allow the voiceover actor to hear their voice during the recording.
Echo	A sound that repeats itself.
Editing	Cutting, replacing, and rearranging parts of an audio to produce a polished audio recording, also improves and corrects errors made during recording.
Ellipsis	Three periods in a row in a script or copy which indicate a significant pause in the copy.
EFX	Term used to refer to sound effects. "SFX" is used as well.
Engineer	The person who operates the audio equipment during an audio recording session.

Equalization	A process for emphasizing some sounds and deemphasizing others in an audio recording.
Exponential	A relationship where a change in value changes in proportion to the current value.
Eye-brain-mouth coordination	The ability to read on a page effectively and convincingly.
Fade	Increase or decrease the volume of sound.
Fade in/fade out	Turning your head toward or away from the microphone.
False start	When a voiceover actor makes an error at the beginning of making an audio recording.
FCC	Federal Communications Commission.
Feedback	High pitched sound, often cause by headphones getting too close to the microphone.
File name extension	A suffix of 3-4 letters added at the end of a file that identifies the type of file format. For example: MP3 format
Filter	A sound effect that lets some sounds come through and blocks others out.
Fish-bowl effect	When a voiceover actor cannot hear what the engineer is saying, and the engineer cannot hear the voiceover talent.
FLAC	An open source compressed audio format.
Foley	A special sound stage used to record sound effect to match the video; for example adding walking sounds, hands clapping, furniture moving.
Franchised	Description of talent agents who adopt SAG-AFTRA guidelines for working with talent.
Frequency	The pitch of sound.
Front bed/back bed	When the announcer is heard at the beginning of the commercial jingle/ when the announcer is heard at the end of a commercial jingle.
FTP	File Transfer Protocol—method used to send data to the public.
Gain	How much a signal or audio is amplified—roughly the loudness.

Gig	A job, a booking.
Go up for	To audition or be considered for a voiceover or acting job.
Gobos	Partitions that can be set up around an actor to absorb sound.
Good pipes	A voiceover actor with a strong, resonant, flexible voice.
Hard sell	High pressure sales technique, characterized by a loud, driving, fast paced speaking style—does not take no for an answer.
Harmonic	A sound that contains a mix of different frequencies.
Harmonizer	Device used to change the pitch of the voice upward—make the pitch higher.
Headroom	The difference between the peak level of the audio track and point where the audio sound is distorted or clipped.
Headset	Headphones.
High-pass filter	A filter that lets high frequencies through.
High speed dub	A copy of a tape or CD recorded at several times the normal speed.
Highs	High frequency voice.
Hold	When a potential client asks a voiceover talent to hold a time slot before formally booking a job.
Holding fee	The fee paid by a potential client so that a voiceover talent will hold the time slot to do the project.
Home recording	Recording from an in-home studio instead of in an outside recording booth.
Home studio	A recording space set up in a voiceover actor's home, for auditions and project work.
Hook	The start of a voiceover read that immediately grabs the attention.
Hot	On—a microphone that is on is called a hot mic.
House demo	A voiceover recording that contains samples of an agent's roster of talent.
Hz	The hertz is the derived unit of frequency in the International System of Units, defined as one cycle per second.

In the can	When voiceover production is complete and ready to be submitted and used.
Inflection	Emphasizing a particular point in a script by increasing or lowering the pitch of specific words or phrases.
In-house	A voiceover production that is created by the client at the client's facilities.
ISDN	Integrated Service for Digital Network; communications protocols to transmit digital signals for voice, video, and data, all at once over a telephone network.
IVR	Interactive Voice Response.
Jack	A socket connector for inserting a plug; for example, connecting headphones and other audio devices.
Jingle	A short musical piece used in a commercial.
KBPS	Kilobit—a unit of data transfer rate of 1000 bits per second.
kHz	Kilohertz—1000 Hz.
LAME	Software that converts audio to MP3 format.
LAN	Local area network.
Latency	A delay between an audio signal being sent and received.
Laundry list	An itemization of points in the copy or script--benefits of a particular party.
Lay it down	Let's record.
Lay out	Do not speak for a particular portion of a voiceover recording.
Level	To set the voice at the optimum point. The voiceover actor will be asked to read the script at the level they intend to read the copy.
Library music	Collection of prerecorded music selections that is used for voiceover recording when the client does not have or want to spend money on original compositions.
Line cue	The last portion of the last line before the voice actor's cue begins.

Line level	The strength of an audio signal used to transmit analog data between audio components such as CDs, DVDs, and TVs.
Line reading	When a director or producer tells a voiceover actor how they want the line in the script or copy to be read.
Linear	A simple one-to-one relationship—a straight line.
Live tag	The copy delivered at the end of a commercial—common in radio.
Local	The union in a particular jurisdiction.
Looping	Recording or rerecording audio dialogue on previously filmed video.
Lossy	An audio format that does not lose information or data when compressed.
Low-pass filter	A process that lets low frequencies (bass) through.
Lows	The low frequency of a voice—bass frequency.
Major markets	In the voiceover industry the main centers of commercial activity are New York, Chicago, and Los Angeles.
Marking copy	Pencil marks over and below and around words in script or copy designating where the voice actor should change pitch, rate, pace, or emphasis.
Master	The original recording.
Metadata	Additional information about an audio or digital file.
Mic	Microphone.
Microphone preamp	Device used to amplify the voltage to a higher level.
Milking	Stretching a word or moment out as much as possible to get every bit of meaning or emphasis out of it.
Mix	Blending voice, music, and background sounds for a complete project.
Mixing board	Electronic equipment or device used to blend voice, music, and background into a final recording product.
Monitors	Loudspeakers in the control room.
Monologues	A script or copy written or to be delivered by one actor.

Mouth noise	The sounds the mouth makes: pops, click, smacks, and the like that occur because of dry mouth.
Moment before	The event that occurs before the beginning of a scene that provides motivation for the actor's approach to the copy.
MP2	Audio format used for broadcast.
MP3	Audio format used for transmitting audio over the Internet.
MP3 CDs	A type of CD that contains only MP3 data.
Multiples	A script with three or more characters in it.
Multitrack	A device that can play several different tracks at once.
Music bed	The music soundtrack that will go underneath the voice audio.
Narrator	The person who tells the story or drives the storyline, leads the audience through the information that the client wants to convey.
Niche market	A specific segment of the market, appealing to a particular audience or promoting a specific product or type of product.
Noise floor	The level of normal background noise.
Non-union	A job for a client or employer that is not a signatory to the SAG-AFTRA agreement.
Off-camera	When only the actor's voice is heard, and the actor is not seen on screen.
On mic/off mic	Speaking directly into the microphone.
Outtake	A take of an audio or video that is not used or approved for use.
Over scale	Payment for work which is above the SAG-AFTRA rate.
Overlapping	When a voice actor or talent starts their line before another actor has finished their line.
Over-the-top	When the actor is asked to essentially overact—make the script reading as broadly acted and large as possible.
Pace	The speed at which an actor reads the copy.
Paper noise	Sound picked up by the microphone when the voice actor or talent moves or turns the pages of a script.

Patch	To make an audio and digital connection for broadcasting.
Paymaster	A payroll company or service that takes payment from the client or employer and pays the talent.
Phasing	When sound reverberates off surfaces and creates distortions in the audio recording.
Phonemes	Units of sounds used to make words.
Phones	Short version of headphones.
Pick-up	A re-recording of a section of audio often to correct an error or to provide an alternative outcome.
Pick-up session	An additional opportunity to re-record a section of an audio product— providing another opportunity to make corrections.
Pitch	The vocal level at which an actor speaks.
Placement	Where the microphone is positioned when an actor is speaking.
Playback	Listening to audio that has been recorded.
Plosive	Consonant sounds that cause a popping sound when captured by the microphone.
Plus ten	When the agent agrees to add 10% to the voiceover talent's contract to cover the agent's 10% fee.
Pop	Plosive sound made when certain consonant sounds are made. (P, T, K, D, G, and B).
Pop filter	A nylon filter or foam cover over a microphone used to keep plosive sounds from reaching the microphone and being picked up.
Popping	Plosive sounds made by speaking certain consonants that are picked up by the microphone.
Post-production	The last step in finalizing a film or video process such as dubbing.
Pre-life/pre-scene	The backstory for an actor's character, sometimes called preceding circumstances.

Problem-Solution	A common rubric for commercials where the consumer is presented with a problem that the product then solves.
Producer	The person responsible for creating the voiceover product; often this person may also be the director.
Promo	A commercial produced by radio stations that seeks to make the public aware of upcoming programming.
Protection	An extra take of an audio or film project to ensure that there is a useable copy of the work in case something happens to the original version. The term "safety" is sometimes used as well.
PSA	Public Service Announcement.
Punch	Reading a word with greater intensity to emphasize the word.
Punch-in	Joining and connecting segments of an audio recording—used when splicing together corrections in audio.
RAW	Audio file format used for storing uncompressed audio.
Read	The style and quality of a voiceover actor's performance of a script.
Real person	When a voiceover actor's performance of the script indicates that the actor uses and endorses the product being sold.
Real-time	The actual time it takes for an action or event to take place.
Red book	16-bit 44100Hz—the most widely used standard for recording audio on CD.
Released	When a voiceover actor is eliminated from consideration for a voiceover job.
Residuals	Payments made to actors and talent beyond the payment for the recording or filming time, based on a union or other agreement for payment based on subsequent use.
Resonance	The quality of a voice reflecting the way in which sound reverberates in the vocal instrument of a voiceover actor.

Re-use	The amount being paid to a voiceover actor based on when the spot or commercial is re-run.
Reverb	A kind of echo.
Room tone	The sound in a room.
Run-through	Rehearsing copy or a script before recording it.
S.A.S.E.	Self-Addressed Stamped Envelope.
SAG-AFTRA	Screen Actors Guild-American Federation of Television and Radio Actors. The national union representing actors, announcers, broadcast journalists, dancers, DJs, news writers, news editors, program hosts, puppeteers, recording artists, singers, stunt performers, voiceover artists, and other media professionals.
Scale	The minimum rate set by SAG-AFTRA for work.
Scale plus 10	The extra 10% paid to the actor or talent's agent on the work.
Scratch track	A rough version of an audio or video track created by an ad agency or production company.
Series of three	A set of words or lines which should be recorded with different levels and pitches.
Session	The time an actor or voiceover talent is scheduled to record.
Session fee	The fee paid to the voiceover actor or talent for the time spent in the recording studio recording the spot.
Shave	To cut down the amount of time it takes to do a read.
Sibilance	A prominent and noticeable "S" sound made when speaking.
Sides	Script.
Signatory	A production company, producer, or agency that has signed an agreement with SAG-AFTRA to work with union talent, pay union scale, and abide by the terms and conditions of employment required for union workers.
Single	Monologue.

Slate	When the actor states at a minimum their name and perhaps the role being sought in their own voice and personality at the beginning or end of an audition.
Smile	Physically smiling when reading adds a friendly, approachable sound to the read. You can literally hear the smile in the voice of the actor.
SOT	Sound on Tape—a sound or noise from the script that is not spoken by the voiceover actor.
Sound effects	Sounds often added to a video or audio performance to enhance the realism or dramatic nature of a piece. The effects can range from the addition of footsteps to imaginary sounds as laser swords. See also EFX.
Specs	Specifications for the script—how the script should be read.
Spectrum	Sound described in frequencies.
Spokesperson	A voice actor or talent hired to represent a brand or product over the course of a contractual agreement.
Spot	A commercial advertisement.
Stair stepping	Increasing or decreasing the pitch over a series of words.
Stand	The item used to hold the voiceover copy in the recording booth.
Station ID	An announcement identifying the call letters of a radio station.
Steps	Increasing the energy on a long list of words or terms.
Storyboard	A producer or art director's illustrated vision of a TV commercial—often mocked up on large boards.
Studio	The facility where voiceover work is recorded.
Sweeps	Period when TV and radio ratings are measured.
Sync	Matching a voice to video.
Taft-Hartley	A labor law that governs the activities of labor unions.
Tag	Information at the end of the commercial that provides legal information.
Take	Recording of a specific copy.
Talent	The actor or person who will be doing the voiceover performance.

Talkback	The button in the recording and engineering booth that allows the talent and the engineer to speak without either leaving their booths.
Tease	Introductory line used to promote interest.
Tempo	Speed at which an audio script is spoken by a voiceover artist. Speed may vary.
Three-in-a-row	Performing a line or phrase multiple times to identify alternative versions.
Tight	Not a lot of time—things having to take place in a compressed amount of time.
Time	The length of the spot.
Time code	The digital value associated with a recording—assists with editing because it is the way that specific moments in a film are isolated.
Tone	A specific sound or social posture.
Track	Audio recording.
Trailer	Short clip or video promoting an upcoming film or television programming.
Trigger	A stimulus, signal, catalyst, or reminder that prompts an emotional response from an actor.
Undercutting	Throwing away a line, deemphasizing a line by not speaking it at full volume, or speaking it very quickly so that it is barely understood or mumbled.
Units	A factor in calculating residuals based on the total number of subscribers to a network.[115]
Use fee	A fee paid to a performer over and above the session fee, when the commercial or other spot is aired.
Value added	Words or expressions in script or copy that indicate that the customer is getting an added benefit at no additional cost or free.

---

[115] "What Are the Payments for Cable Use? | SAG-AFTRA."

V-O	Voice over
Voiceover coach	A trainer or teacher who helps voice actors and talent master the specific skills for approaching a script, perfect the vocal instrument and vocal style. Voiceover coaches also provide technical advice on home studio set-up, and marketing and networking opportunities as well.
Voiceover talent	A person who speaks or performs commercial, animation, training video, books, or device scripts copy.
Voice print	Representation of the vocal sound that can be seen on a monitor when using audio recording software.
Voice seeker	Client or business looking to hire a voiceover actor or talent.
VU meter	Device on a soundboard that measures the level of sound.
Watermark	In audio, sounds or tones mixed into a recording that seek to prevent the product from being used without payment or authorization.
WAV	Format used by windows for creating an audio CD.
Wild line	A line from a script that is read several different times in several different ways.
Wild spot	When a commercial runs or airs on several stations that are not connected and not a sponsor for a program. Fee paid is based on the units assigned to the market or cities in which the commercial airs over a 13-week period. Unit value is determined by the number of subscribers or households for each station.
Windows Direct Sound	A Windows interface or connector between audio recording programs such as Audacity.
Windows WASPI	Most recent Windows interface for Audacity.
Windscreen	A pop filter.
WMA	An audio format for windows.
Woodshed	To rehearse copy or script aloud.
Wrap	The end. Finished, done.

| Zephyr | A device that is used to connect your recording universally compatible to other digital networks. |

Sample Voiceover Business Startup Budget

Voiceover is a business. It makes sense to start your voiceover journey as a business from the very beginning. That is why I have included a template for a simple budget. Having a budget helps provide you with a focus and priorities. In most instances when you start a new business, experts advise you to start by saving money to build your dream. Your approach to starting your voiceover business should be the same. The good news is that a relatively modest amount of saving for your voiceover business should get you off to a good start.

The other benefit of using this budget is that it helps to limit the risk of starting a new business. It will discourage you from dipping into your regular household budget and potentially destabilizing your day-to-day finances. Working with a simple budget can also help discourage impulse buying. Buying according to a plan helps resist the urge to buy the latest and flashiest new gadget or equipment out of sequence or long before that investment can pay off in revenue from voiceover jobs.

We have discussed approaching your voiceover journey in phases. If money is tight and you are anxious to get started, you could start out with some of the cost-free aspects of your plan while you are saving money for the next stage. In the best-case scenario, I would recommend setting aside around **$5,000** to be able to comfortably invest in the things you need to get your voiceover business off to a good start.

The model budget included in this Guide brings you in at under **$4,000.**[116] This budget, however, does cut some significant corners, like by waiting to invest in a more professional home studio until you have had significant training. It is also important to note that it likely will not be long before you will need to upgrade your home studio set-up. Once you start to audition and get work, it is imperative that you have a reasonably well-treated home studio space where you can produce a high quality, professional product.

____

[116] Compared to the costs of other startup businesses, saving $4,000-$5000 is within reach, particularly if you are creative. How much, even a little, can you save from each paycheck (save without missing it)? Instead of gifts, can you ask family and friends to contribute toward your dream? If you are already an actor, can you earmark any residual checks that come in for your new voiceover business? In a gig economy, could picking up a part-time gig help propel you more quickly to your dreams? In an uncertain economy, I would be reluctant to dip into existing savings—but in the end it's your choice as to the amount of grit, energy, and hustle you bring to this new adventure in your life.

What will it cost you to get your voiceover business up and running? I have listed the main costs and left space to add any additional costs specific to you.

You can, of course, choose to start with a larger budget. My goal here is to provide you with an example of a moderate to conservative spend to ease you comfortably into the voiceover business. These are ballpark figures—but they should give you an idea of what it takes to start.

Budget

STARTUP EXPENSES		
Training and Development	**AMOUNT**	
Voiceover coach	$1,500.00	
Online voiceover website memberships	$0.00	
Workshops and class	$0.00	
Other	$0.00	
Total	**$1,500.00**	
Voiceover Equipment Set-up	**AMOUNT**	
Microphone	$200.00	
Condenser	$300.00	
Computer and computer software	$0.00	Free Software: Audacity
Home studio - DIY	$100.00	Treating a space in your home with blankets and pillows to start out.

Other	$0.00	
Total	**$600.00**	
Marketing and Promotion	**AMOUNT**	
Demo taping production	$1,200.00	
Branding consultant or agent	$0.00	
Website	$0.00	
Headshot	$500.00	
Business management tools—Voice overview	$96.00	
Other	$0.00	
Total	**$1,796.00**	
LOCATION AND ADMIN EXPENSES	**AMOUNT**	
Studio/Office rental	$0.00	
Utility deposits	$0.00	
Legal and accounting fees	$0.00	
Prepaid insurance	$0.00	
Other	$0.00	
Total	**$0.00**	

ADDITIONAL ADVERTISING AND PROMOTIONAL EXPENSES	AMOUNT	
Advertising	$0.00	
Printing	$0.00	
Travel/entertainment	$0.00	
Other/additional categories	$0.00	
Total	**$0.00**	
OTHER EXPENSES	**AMOUNT**	
Other expense 1	$0.00	
Other expense 2	$0.00	
Total	**$0.00**	
SUMMARY STATEMENT		
Total	**$0.00**	
STARTUP EXPENSES	**TOTALS**	
Training and development	$1,500.00	
Voiceover equipment set-up	$600.00	
Total	**$2,100.00**	Phases I and II
Marketing and promotion	$1,796.00	Phase III

Location/administration expenses	$0.00	
Additional advertising/promotional expenses	$0.00	
Other expenses	$0.00	
Total	**$3,896.00**	
Notes		

Sample Action Plan

Objective	Task	How will you know you succeed?	Time Frame	Resources needed

Bibliography

7 Great Teachers to Kick-Start Your Voiceover Career. Available at: https://www.backstage.com/magazine/article/great-teachers-kick-start-voiceover-career-9507/ (Accessed: 22 September 2020).

7 Tips for Working with Voice-Over in Corporate Video Projects (no date). Available at: https://www.premiumbeat.com/blog/7-tips-voice-over-corporate-video/ (Accessed: 9 September 2020).

9 Types of Voiceover Work (no date). Available at: https://www.backstage.com/magazine/article/9-types-of-voiceover-work-70259/ (Accessed: 4 September 2020).

10 elements of powerful podcast promos (no date). Available at: https://theaudacitytopodcast.com/10-elements-of-powerful-podcast-promos-tap141/ (Accessed: 4 September 2020).

17 Best Voice Over Microphones for a Home Recording Studio: The Complete List (2020 Update) (no date). Available at: https://myelearningworld.com/10-quality-voice-over-microphones-for-a-home-recording-studio/ (Accessed: 25 September 2020).

23 Black Actors Who Voiced Your Favorite Cartoon Characters | HuffPost (no date b). Available at: https://www.huffpost.com/entry/black-actors-cartoon-characters_n_560e9be0e4b0af3706e06b23 (Accessed: 16 September 2020).

(129) Anne Ganguzza Corporate / Industrial Narration Demo - YouTube (no date). Available at: https://www.youtube.com/watch?v=TtjUtOqkxOs (Accessed: 9 September 2020).

(129) Marc Scott Corporate Narration Voice Over Demo - YouTube (no date). Available at: https://www.youtube.com/watch?v=B1nOGTdy3A8 (Accessed: 9 September 2020).

(190) Lessac Structural Vowel Voice Lesson - YouTube (no date). Available at: https://www.youtube.com/watch?v=tJZyIlrTsz8 (Accessed: 17 September 2020).

(193) Pattern Interruption and the Musicality of Voice Over - YouTube (no date). Available at: https://www.youtube.com/watch?v=OBZBtqF64JA (Accessed: 17 September 2020).

(374) How to Turn a Closet into a Vocal Booth with Ronnie Rokk Smith - YouTube (no date a). Available at: https://www.youtube.com/watch?v=EZieBUAHlv0 (Accessed: 9 October 2020).

'2019 Washington-Mid Atlantic Regional Commercials Code 8_20.pdf' (no date). Available at: https://www.sagaftra.org/files/2019WashingtonMid-AtlanticRegionalCommercialsCode8_20.pdf (Accessed: 13 October 2020).

A Guide to Microphone Types, Polar Patterns, and Placement | Home | Reverb News (no date a). Available at: https://reverb.com/news/home-recording-basics-iii-a-guide-to-microphone-types-and-placement?utm_source=google&utm_medium=cpc&utm_campaign=244170686&utm_content=campaignid=244170686_adgroupid=19499674646_keyword=_device=c_adposition=_matchtype=b_creative=432737242454&gclid=CjwKCAjwh7H7BRBBEiwAPXjadhhTRH-NwyOM-38ISiQtQySd6w42q9LJduDdmUKUhJnsjh6oUXx4VRoCn2gQAvD_BwE (Accessed: 24 September 2020).

A short history of the audiobook, 20 years after the first portable digital audio device (2017a) *PBS NewsHour*. Available at: https://www.pbs.org/newshour/arts/a-short-history-of-the-audiobook-20-years-after-the-first-portable-digital-audio-device (Accessed: 25 August 2020).

About Voice Forward & Anna Garduño (no date). Available at: http://voiceforward.com/about/ (Accessed: 30 August 2020).

Adjunct Faculty at The Acting Studio - New York - The Acting Studio - New York, LLC (no date). Available at: https://www.actingstudio.com/acting-studio-faculty/adjunct (Accessed: 22 September 2020).

ADR Voice Over Jobs - Find Out All About How to Get ADR Work (no date a). Available at: https://www.gravyforthebrain.com/adr-voice-over-jobs/ (Accessed: 25 August 2020).

ADR Work Requires Skill and Determination (no date). Available at: https://www.backstage.com/magazine/article/adr-work-requires-skill-determination-56295/ (Accessed: 10 September 2020).

Agos, Chris (no date) *Voice Over Startup Guide: How to Land Your First VO Job.*

Alburger, J. (2019) *The Art of Voice Acting: The Craft and Business of Performing for Voiceover.* CRC Press.

An Expressive Voice, How to Use Your Voice Effectively (no date). Available at: http://totalcommunicator.com/vol2_3/voicemessage.html (Accessed: 16 September 2020).

Anime Voice Over Jobs - Find How to Get into Anime Voice Over (no date). Available at: https://www.gravyforthebrain.com/anime-voice-over-jobs/ (Accessed: 25 August 2020).

AQA | Drama | Subject content | Guidance on theatrical skills (no date). Available at: https://www.aqa.org.uk/subjects/drama/gcse/drama-8261/subject-content/guidance-on-theatrical-skills (Accessed: 15 September 2020).

Audacity Manual (no date). Available at: https://manual.audacityteam.org/ (Accessed: 8 October 2020).

Audacity Versions - Audacity Wiki (no date). Available at: https://wiki.audacityteam.org/wiki/Audacity_Versions#compatibility (Accessed: 8 October 2020).

Audiobook Auditions: Have Fun and Stand Out! - Such A Voice (no date). Available at: https://www.suchavoice.com/2020/09/17/audiobook-auditions-have-fun-and-stand-out/?inf_contact_key=ad22d8e7f5ff9c035d1d88643becc8d1cc0558ed5d4c28cbfab114022b1ec50d (Accessed: 19 September 2020).

Audiobook Performance Masterclass (2017). Available at: https://www.youtube.com/watch?v=booccER-4yo (Accessed: 4 September 2020).

Audiobook Reviews and Recommendations | AudioFile Magazine (no date). Available at: https://www.audiofilemagazine.com/ (Accessed: 9 September 2020).

Audiobooks | SAG-AFTRA (no date). Available at: https://www.sagaftra.org/audiobooks (Accessed: 9 September 2020).

Audiobooks Featuring Must-Listen Performances | Audible.com (no date a). Available at: https://www.audible.com/ep/best-performances-audiobooks (Accessed: 8 September 2020).

Audiobooks Voice Over Jobs - Find Out All About Audiobook Narration (no date a). Available at: https://www.gravyforthebrain.com/audiobook-voice-over-jobs/ (Accessed: 25 August 2020).

Best PBS Cartoons | List of Animated Kids Shows on PBS (no date a). Available at: https://www.ranker.com/list/best-pbs-cartoons/ranker-tv (Accessed: 13 September 2020).

Blakemore, T. (2015) *Recording Voiceover: The Spoken Word in Media*. CRC Press.

Breaking into the World of Video Game Voiceover (no date a). Available at: https://www.backstage.com/uk/magazine/article/breaking-world-video-game-voiceover-321/ (Accessed: 4 September 2020).

Carrie Olsen – Carrie Olsen Voiceover (no date). Available at: https://carrieolsenvo.com/author/carrieolsenvo/ (Accessed: 22 September 2020).

Carrie Olsen Voiceover – Voiceover talent and voiceover coach (no date). Available at: https://carrieolsenvo.com/ (Accessed: 24 September 2020).

Cartoon Voice Over Jobs - The Fascinating World of Voicing Cartoons (no date). Available at: https://www.gravyforthebrain.com/cartoon-voice-over-jobs/ (Accessed: 25 August 2020).

Cartoon Voice Over Jobs; Here's What You Need to Know - Bunny Studio (no date a). Available at: https://bunnystudio.com/blog/cartoon-voice-over-jobs-heres-what-you-need-to-know/ (Accessed: 23 September 2020).

Copy Reading. How do voice actors make the narration pop? Voice Acting Coach Rachel Alena dishes... (no date). Available at: https://www.rachelalena.com/2017/05/01/voice-acting-coach-2/ (Accessed: 17 September 2020).

Corporate Narration - Brigid Reale & Jace Reale (no date). Available at: https://www.realevoices.com/corporate-narration/ (Accessed: 9 September 2020).

Create a Website with Weebly's Powerful Website Builder (no date). Available at: https://www.weebly.com/websites (Accessed: 11 October 2020).

Creating Your Voice-Over Business Plan (no date). Available at: https://www.suchavoice.com/2016/04/14/5911/ (Accessed: 13 October 2020).

Demo Dos and Don'ts (2003). Available at: https://www.backstage.com/magazine/article/demo-dos-donts-45462/ (Accessed: 14 October 2020).

Diction in Voiceover – The Voice Realm (no date a). Available at: https://www.thevoicerealm.com/blog/diction-in-voiceover/ (Accessed: 17 September 2020).

Do I Need an Agent for Voice Over Work? | Voquent (no date). Available at: https://www.voquent.com/do-i-need-an-agent-for-voice-over-work/ (Accessed: 13 October 2020).

Do you need a Voiceover Agent? | The Voiceover Gurus (no date). Available at: https://voiceover.guru/do-you-need-a-voiceover-agent/ (Accessed: 13 October 2020).

Everything You Need to Know About Promo Voiceover Work (no date a). Available at: https://www.backstage.com/magazine/article/everything-need-know-promo-voiceover-work-1938/ (Accessed: 4 September 2020).

Fan of 'The Simpsons'? Audition for These Animated Projects (no date a). Available at: https://www.backstage.com/magazine/article/the-simpsons-fox-animation-casting-auditions-gigs-71700/?utm_campaign=Daily%20Jobs%20National&utm_medium=email&_hsmi=95092700&_hsenc=p2ANqtz--IhDAbHQK_qIovwjkrn4NcfTOEiy-ft4p--8fTnTScqJvCLqOCn03adJu8ui3QeHwssK9dGqzGS90Zvb-j0nnLtt2RpQ&utm_content=95092700&utm_source=hs_email (Accessed: 13 September 2020).

Female Professional Narration Service for Corporate Videos (no date a). Available at: https://www.debbiegrattan.com/voiceover-services/narration/corporate-videos/ (Accessed: 25 August 2020).

Find a Voice Pro - Voice and Speech Trainers Association (no date). Available at: https://vasta.clubexpress.com/content.aspx?page_id=154&club_id=516524 (Accessed: 21 September 2020).

Find Voice-Over Work & Voice Acting Jobs (Ultimate Guide) (no date). Available at: https://voiceacting101.com/voice-over-work/ (Accessed: 13 October 2020).

Finding + Landing a Voiceover Agent (no date). Available at: https://www.backstage.com/magazine/article/finding-landing-voiceover-agent-1063/ (Accessed: 13 October 2020).

Finding the Natural Rhythm in Voiceover Copy - Peter Drew Voiceovers (no date). Available at: http://www.peterdrewvo.com/articles/finding-the-natural-rhythm-in-voiceover-copy/ (Accessed: 16 September 2020).

Free Voice Over Scripts - Read, Print & Practice Ready Voice Acting Scripts (no date). Available at: https://www.voiceactorwebsites.com/free-voice-over-scripts/ (Accessed: 11 October 2020).

Free Website Builder | Create a Free Website | Wix.com (no date). Available at: https://www.wix.com/ (Accessed: 11 October 2020).

GarageBand for Windows 10 PC - Download & Install [2020] (no date). Available at: https://garagebandforpcwindows.com/ (Accessed: 8 October 2020).

Get a professional voice over | Bunny Studio Voice (no date). Available at: https://bunnystudio.com/voice/search?purpose=10 (Accessed: 9 September 2020).

Getting a Voice Talent Agent | Voices.com (no date). Available at: https://www.voices.com/help/beginners-guide-to-voice-acting/getting-an-agent (Accessed: 13 October 2020).

Getting an Agent – I Want to Be a Voice Actor! (no date). Available at: https://iwanttobeavoiceactor.com/getting-an-agent/ (Accessed: 13 October 2020).

Glossary - Audacity Manual (no date). Available at: https://manual.audacityteam.org/man/glossary.html (Accessed: 8 October 2020).

Glossary of Voice Acting Terms | Global Voice Acting Academy | Voice Over Coaching & Classes (no date). Available at: https://globalvoiceacademy.com/resources/glossary-of-voice-acting-terms/ (Accessed: 16 September 2020).

Glossary of Voiceover Terms All Actors Should Know (no date). Available at: https://www.backstage.com/magazine/article/must-know-voiceover-terms-7216/ (Accessed: 15 October 2020).

Grammy-winning violinist Joshua Bell delights masses at DC subway concert | PBS NewsHour (no date). Available at: https://www.pbs.org/newshour/arts/grammy-winning-violinist-joshua-bell-takes-another-turn-at-a-subway-concert (Accessed: 26 August 2020).

GVAA Rate Guide | Global Voice Acting Academy | Voice Over Coaching & Classes (no date a). Available at: https://globalvoiceacademy.com/gvaa-rate-guide-2/ (Accessed: 13 October 2020).

Harlan Hogan - Voice overs Narrations Commercials Promos, Chicago Voiceover known around the world (no date). Available at: https://harlanhogan.com/coachList.php (Accessed: 22 September 2020).

Home (no date a). Available at: https://usa.gravyforthebrain.com/#courses (Accessed: 25 August

HOME - Sovas (no date). Available at: https://www.sovas.org/ (Accessed: 23 September 2020).

Home - Voice and Speech Trainers Association (no date). Available at: https://www.vasta.org/content.aspx?sl=1583505933 (Accessed: 21 September 2020).

How I Became a Successful Cartoon Voice Actor | For Talent - Creative Inspiration | Voices.com Blog (no date a). Available at: https://www.voices.com/blog/how-i-became-successful-cartoon-voice-actor/ (Accessed: 1 September 2020).

How it works | Bunny Studio Voice (no date a). Available at: https://bunnystudio.com/voice/how-it-works/ (Accessed: 9 September 2020).

How It Works - Finding Your Perfect Voice Over | Voices.com (no date). Available at: https://www.voices.com/how-it-works (Accessed: 11 October 2020).

How Much Do Voice Actors Make? Voice Actor Salary Goals | Voices.com (no date). Available at: https://www.voices.com/blog/voice-actor-salaries/ (Accessed: 25 August 2020).

How to Be a Video Game Voiceover Artist (no date a). Available at: https://www.backstage.com/magazine/article/video-game-voiceover-artist-5572/ (Accessed: 4 September 2020).

How to Become a Voice Actor for Animation and Cartoon | Voices.com (no date). Available at: https://www.voices.com/blog/how-to-become-cartoon-animation-voice-actor/ (Accessed: 23 September 2020).

How to Do Voice Overs: Everything You Need to Know (no date). Available at: https://www.musicianonamission.com/how-to-do-voice-overs/ (Accessed: 9 September 2020).

How to Find a Great Voiceover Coach (no date a). Available at: https://www.backstage.com/magazine/article/how-to-find-a-great-voiceover-coach-66201/ (Accessed: 22 September 2020).

How to Find and Hire a Voice Actor Online | Voice Over Website (no date). Available at: https://www.thevoicerealm.com/how-to-hire-voice-actors.php (Accessed: 11 October 2020).

How to Find Voiceover Work in E-Learning, Corporate Narration, Audiobooks + Explainer Videos (no date). Available at: https://www.backstage.com/magazine/article/voiceover-e-learning-corporate-narration-audiobooks-explainers-68726/ (Accessed: 9 September 2020).

How to Get a Voice Agent - Tips from a top voice agent. (no date). Available at: https://www.gravyforthebrain.com/how-to-get-a-voice-agent/ (Accessed: 13 October 2020).

How to Make a Voice-Over Demo (no date). Available at: https://www.suchavoice.com/2017/06/09/howtomakeavoiceoverdemo/ (Accessed: 11 October 2020).

How to Master Voiceover Character Skills (no date). Available at: https://usa.gravyforthebrain.com/how-to-master-voiceover-character-skills/ (Accessed: 7 September 2020).

How to Turn a Closet Into a DIY Sound Booth (no date a). Available at: https://www.premiumbeat.com/blog/how-to-turn-a-closet-into-a-diy-sound-booth/ (Accessed: 9 October 2020).

How to Use GarageBand on a Mac - Easy Tips & Pointers | Voices.com (no date). Available at: https://www.voices.com/blog/getting_started_with_garageband/ (Accessed: 8 October 2020).

In a world without voiceovers: What happened to the movie trailer voice? - The Globe and Mail (no date). Available at: https://www.theglobeandmail.com/arts/film/in-a-world-without-voiceovers-what-happened-to-the-movie-trailer-voice/article18806436/ (Accessed: 4 September 2020).

Internet Voice Over Jobs - A Fast Growing Part of The Voice Over Industry (no date). Available at: https://www.gravyforthebrain.com/internet-voice-over-jobs/ (Accessed: 25 August 2020).

IVR Voice Over Jobs - Create an Income by Voicing IVR (no date). Available at: https://www.gravyforthebrain.com/ivr-voice-over-jobs/ (Accessed: 25 August 2020).

Kevin Clay Narrator - Audiobooks (no date). Available at: http://www.kevinclaynarrator.com/ (Accessed: 4 September 2020).

Learn Voiceover Without a Coach – Carrie Olsen Voiceover (no date). Available at: https://carrieolsenvo.com/voice-training/learn-voiceover-without-coach/ (Accessed: 22 September 2020).

Looping and ADR - Bonnie Gillespie (no date a). Available at: https://bonniegillespie.com/looping-and-adr/ (Accessed: 10 September 2020).

Making Money Doing Voice Over | Voices.com (no date). Available at: https://www.voices.com/help/beginners-guide-to-voice-acting/making-money-doing-voice-overs (Accessed: 25 August 2020).

Mazzoleni, L. (no date) 'Do realize that there's more to voice-over than having a good voice,' p. 1.

Melissa Disney (no date). Available at: http://www.melissadisney.com/#melissa (Accessed: 26 August 2020).

Membership Shop (no date). Available at: https://usa.gravyforthebrain.com/membership-shop/ (Accessed: 5 September 2020).

NEW! Online 3 Week ADVANCED VOICEOVER Class with Eileen Schellhorn, Head of Voiceover Division, DDO Artists Agency | Actors Connection (no date). Available at: https://www.actorsconnection.com/classes/2020-10-06-img-2771lnew-online-3-week-advanced-voiceover-class-with-eileen-schellhorn-head-of-voiceover-division-ddo-artists-agency/ (Accessed: 15 September 2020).

News, B. B. C. (no date) *Can 10,000 hours of practice make you an expert? BBC News*. Available at: https://www.bbc.com/news/magazine-26384712 (Accessed: 19 September 2020).

Our Clients - Pro Podcast Solutions (no date). Available at: https://propodcastsolutions.com/clients/ (Accessed: 4 September 2020).

Pattern Interruption and the Musicality of Voice Over - vo2gogo.com (no date). Available at: https://www.vo2gogo.com/pattern-interruption-and-the-musicality-of-voice-over/ (Accessed: 17 September 2020).

Pearls Before Breakfast: Can one of the nation's great musicians cut through the fog of a D.C. rush hour? Let's find out. - The Washington Post (no date). Available at: https://www.washingtonpost.com/ (Accessed: 26 August 2020).

Pitch: Public Speaking/Speech Communication (no date). Available at: https://lumen.instructure.com/courses/218897/pages/linkedtext54274 (Accessed: 15 September 2020).

Planning Your Voice-Over Demos | Voices.com (no date). Available at: https://www.voices.com/help/beginners-guide-to-voice-acting/planning-your-demos (Accessed: 9 October 2020).

Podcast Voice Overs - Pro Podcast Solutions (no date). Available at: https://propodcastsolutions.com/podcast-voice-overs/ (Accessed: 4 September 2020).

Practice Voice Acting - Build a Powerful Voice Using These Techniques (no date a). Available at: https://www.gravyforthebrain.com/practice-voice-acting/ (Accessed: 9 September 2020).

Preston, Marc (no date) *How to Choose a Reputable Voiceover Coach/Consultant*. Available at: https://marcprestonconsulting.com/choosingacoach/

Pro Podcast Solutions Podcast Editing and Consulting (no date). Available at: https://propodcastsolutions.com/ (Accessed: 4 September 2020).

Radio Voice Over Jobs - Learn About the Work Voice Overs Do in Radio (no date). Available at: https://www.gravyforthebrain.com/radio-voice-over-jobs/ (Accessed: 25 August 2020).

Read This Before You Hire a Voice Over Coach - Bunny Studio (no date a). Available at: https://bunnystudio.com/blog/read-this-before-you-hire-a-voice-over-coach/ (Accessed: 22 September 2020).

Reading a Script | Voice Over Tips & Resources — The Voice Shop (no date). Available at: http://www.voiceshopcoaching.com/reading-a-script (Accessed: 17 September 2020).

Register – The African American voice actor database (no date). Available at: https://www.aavadb.com/profile/register/ (Accessed: 14 October 2020).

Schultz, T. (no date) 'Breaking into Today's Voice Over Industry with Connectivism,' p. 15.

Search Voice Actors by Voice Over Category | Voices.com (no date a). Available at: https://www.voices.com/voice-actors/category (Accessed: 11 October 2020).

Setting Up a Home VO Studio? Here's What You MUST Know. (no date). Available at: https://www.backstage.com/magazine/article/setting-home-vo-studio-must-know-5341/ (Accessed: 9 October 2020).

Siegel, Cecelia (no date a) *Voiceover Achiever: Brand Your VO Career. Change Your Life.* Available at: https://www.amazon.com/Voiceover-Achiever-Brand-career-Change/dp/0692991808.

Siegel, Cecelia (no date b) *Voiceover Achiever: Brand Your VO Career. Change Your Life.* Celia Siegel (January 15, 2018).

Smooth Narrations: Rhythm & flow for voice actors from expert voice talent coach (no date). Available at: https://www.rachelalena.com/2018/03/22/smooth-narrations/ (Accessed: 16 September 2020).

Some Voice Over Film Examples for your Entertainment - Bunny Studio (no date). Available at: https://bunnystudio.com/blog/some-voice-over-film-examples-for-your-entertainment/ (Accessed: 11 September 2020).

Speed Reading - Why Voiceovers Need to Master This Art (no date a). Available at: https://usa.gravyforthebrain.com/the-art-of-speed-reading/ (Accessed: 10 September 2020).

Sun King Media: A Cautionary Tale for New Voiceovers About VO Scams (no date). Available at: https://usa.gravyforthebrain.com/sun-king-media-new-voiceovers-vo-scams/ (Accessed: 10 September 2020).

Testimonials (no date). Available at: https://www.voschoollaunch.com/testimonials.html (Accessed: 4 September 2020).

The 4 Most Important Elements of Your Voice (no date). Available at: https://www.fastcompany.com/3047183/the-4-most-important-elements-of-your-voice (Accessed: 16 September 2020).

The 7 Pillars of Voiceover Technique | Voice Over Gurus Blog (no date a). Available at: http://www.voiceovergurus.com/guru_blog/?p=348 (Accessed: 16 September 2020).

The Art of Voice-Over Cadences - Such A Voice (no date a). Available at: https://www.suchavoice.com/2019/03/07/the-art-of-voice-over-cadences/ (Accessed: 16 September 2020).

The Best Audio Editing Software for 2020 | PCMag (no date). Available at: https://www.pcmag.com/picks/the-best-audio-editing-software?test_uuid=01jrZgWNXhmA3ocG7ZHXevj&test_variant=b (Accessed: 8 October 2020).

The Best Voiceover Articles, Ideas, and Tips on Marketing | Voice Over Gurus Blog (no date). Available at: http://www.voiceovergurus.com/guru_blog/?p=354#comment-255 (Accessed: 16 September 2020).

The Complete Guide to Improving Vocal Control - Ramsey Voice Studio (no date a). Available at: https://ramseyvoice.com/vocal-control/ (Accessed: 17 September 2020).

The Importance of IVR Phone System and On Hold Voice Over | Voices.com Blog (no date). Available at: https://www.voices.com/blog/telephone-system-voice-over/ (Accessed: 26 August 2020).

The Life of a Voice-Over Artist (no date). Available at: https://www.suchavoice.com/2016/04/19/lifeofavoiceoverartist/?inf_contact_key=5d3e81030759643c62d37e27eaa89b27f651f238aa2edbb9c8b7cff03e0b16a0 (Accessed: 13 September 2020).

Thompson, S. A. (2014a) *In a world without voiceovers: What happened to the movie trailer voice? The Globe and Mail.* Available at: https://www.theglobeandmail.com/arts/film/in-a-world-without-voiceovers-what-happened-to-the-movie-trailer-voice/article18806436/ (Accessed: 4 September 2020).

Top 10 Audio Recording Software to Capture Your Voice Easily (no date). Available at: https://filmora.wondershare.com/best-audio-recording-software.html (Accessed: 8 October 2020).

Trailer Addict - Movie Trailers (no date). Available at: https://www.traileraddict.com/ (Accessed: 26 August 2020).

Types of Vocal Timbre | Music to Your Home (no date a). Available at: https://www.musictoyourhome.com/blog/types-of-vocal-timbre/ (Accessed: 19 September 2020).

Video Game Voice Over Jobs - Get Started in This Exciting Industry (no date a). Available at: https://www.gravyforthebrain.com/video-game-voice-over-jobs/ (Accessed: 25 August 2020).

Videos | Audiobook Creation Exchange Blog (ACX) (no date). Available at: https://blog.acx.com/category/videos/ (Accessed: 4 September 2020).

VO School | Free Listening on SoundCloud (no date). Available at: https://soundcloud.com/voschool (Accessed: 4 September 2020).

Vocal Control | Musical U (no date). Available at: https://www.musical-u.com/modules/singing/vocal-control/ (Accessed: 17 September 2020).

Voice Acting Academy (no date) *Get Started in Voiceover.* Available at: https://voiceacting.com/training/get-started-in-voiceover/

Voice Acting/Basic Voice Acting Skills - Wikiversity (no date). Available at: https://soundcloud.com/voschool (Accessed: 16 September 2020).

Voice Over Business - How to Create a Thriving VO Business (no date). Available at: https://www.gravyforthebrain.com/start-voice-over-business/ (Accessed: 13 October 2020).

Voice Over Casting - Voice Talent Jobs | Edge Studio (no date). Available at: https://www.edgestudio.com/careerbuilding.htm (Accessed: 26 August 2020).

Voice Over Demo Scripts: Everything You Need to Know (no date). Available at: https://bunnystudio.com/blog/voice-over-demo-scripts-everything-you-need-to-know/ (Accessed: 24 September 2020).

Voice Over Gurus Blog | The Online VoiceOver Community (no date). Available at: http://www.voiceovergurus.com/guru_blog/ (Accessed: 16 September 2020).

Voice Over Marketing Tips from Producers Who Hire Voice Talent (no date). Available at: https://www.debbiegrattan.com/blog/voice-marketing-tips-from-producers/ (Accessed: 9 October 2020).

Voice Over Sample Scripts | Edge Studio (no date). Available at: https://www.edgestudio.com/voice-over-scripts (Accessed: 11 October 2020).

Voice Over Sample Scripts - Free Demo & Practice Scripts | Voices.com (no date). Available at: https://www.voices.com/blog/voice-over-sample-scripts/ (Accessed: 11 October 2020).

Voice Over Training and Demo Production | Such A Voice (no date). Available at: https://www.suchavoice.com/ (Accessed: 7 September 2020).

Voice Over Xtra (no date). Available at: https://www.voiceoverxtra.com/index.htm#news (Accessed: 22 September 2020).

Voice quality (no date). Available at: https://www2.ims.uni-stuttgart.de/EGG/page2.htm (Accessed: 17 September 2020).

Voiceover 101 (2019). Available at: https://www.backstage.com/magazine/article/voiceover-training-5077/ (Accessed: 4 September 2020).

Voice-Over Guides (no date). Available at: https://voiceacting101.com/voice-over-acting-guides/ (Accessed: 15 September 2020).

'Voice-Over Narration: What is it? How Much Does it Cost?' (2018) *Debbie Grattan Voiceover Talent*, 11 January. Available at: https://www.debbiegrattan.com/blog/voice-over-narration-cost-definition/ (Accessed: 25 August 2020).

Voice-Over Rates: Knowing Your Value and What to Charge (no date b). Available at: https://www.suchavoice.com/2018/05/24/voice-over-rates/ (Accessed: 26 August 2020).

Voiceoverview - Voice Over CRM and Voice Actor Business Management Tool (no date a). Available at: https://voiceoverview.com/pricing (Accessed: 14 October 2020).

Weebly Pricing - Compare Website Builder Plans and Pricing (no date). Available at: https://www.weebly.com/pricing (Accessed: 11 October 2020).

WellSaid Labs – Products (no date). Available at: https://wellsaidlabs.com/products (Accessed: 9 September 2020).

What are the important qualities of a voice-over artist? (no date). Available at: https://www.alphatrad.com/news/characteristics-voice-over-artists (Accessed: 16 September 2020).

What are the payments for cable use? | SAG-AFTRA (no date). Available at: https://www.sagaftra.org/what-are-payments-cable-use (Accessed: 23 October 2020).

What It's Like to Work on Video Games, According to 'Mass Effect' VO Actor Jennifer Hale (no date). Available at: https://www.backstage.com/magazine/article/act-video-games-jennifer-hale-mass-effect-43991/ (Accessed: 7 September 2020).

What Voice Actors Need to Know About 'Voice Matching' (no date a). Available at: https://www.backstage.com/magazine/article/match-game-1-63931/ (Accessed: 4 September 2020).

What Voice Actors Should Know About Looping, ADR + Walla (no date). Available at: https://www.backstage.com/magazine/article/what-voice-actors-should-know-about-looping-adr-walla-69048/ (Accessed: 10 September 2020).

What's ADR in Film and Why is it Important? (no date). Available at: https://nofilmschool.com/what-is-adr-in-film (Accessed: 26 August 2020).

When working on an animated film, do the actors voice their part after the animation is done, or is the animation done before any voice work is done? - Quora (no date). Available at: https://www.quora.com/When-working-on-an-animated-film-do-the-actors-voice-their-part-after-the-animation-is-done-or-is-the-animation-done-before-any-voice-work-is-done (Accessed: 23 September 2020).

Wix Pricing Information | Upgrade to a Premium Plan | Wix.com (no date) Available at: https://www.wix.com/upgrade/website (Accessed: 11 October 2020).

"4 of the Best Cities for Film and TV Production Crews | Casting Agencies Directory." Accessed December 6, 2020. https://www.castingagenciesdirectory.com/blog/4-of-the-best-cities-for-film-and-tv-production-crews

"17 Examples of Fabulous Explainer Videos." Accessed December 17, 2020. https://blog.hubspot.com/marketing/explainer-videos

"38 Must Know Voiceover Terms." Accessed February 16, 2021. https://www.backstage.com/magazine/article/must-know-voiceover-terms-7216/

"(59) Voicing for the Background | Film Jobs with Loop Group West - YouTube." Accessed December 6, 2020. https://www.youtube.com/watch?v=BO1ivoU8GDc

"(190) Lessac Structural Vowel Voice Lesson - YouTube." Accessed September 17, 2020. https://www.youtube.com/watch?v=tJZyIlrTsz8

"2017 Global Voice Over Market Report | Voices.Com." Accessed October 30, 2020. https://www.voices.com/company/press/reports/2017-global-voice-over-market-report

"2017 Voice Over Trends Report | Voices.Com." Accessed October 30, 2020. https://www.voices.com/company/press/reports/2017-voice-over-trends-report

"2019 Voice-over Industry Report | Voice-Over Freelance." Accessed October 30, 2020. https://voiceoverfreelance.com/2019-voice-over-industry-report/

"A Guide to Microphone Types, Polar Patterns, and Placement | Home Recording Basics | Reverb News." Accessed September 24, 2020. https://reverb.com/news/home-recording-basics-iii-a-guide-to-microphone-types-and-placement?utm_source=google&utm_medium=cpc&utm_campaign=244170686&utm_content=campaignid=244170686_adgroupid=19499674646_keyword=_device=c_adposition=_matchtype=b_creative=432737242454&gclid=CjwKCAjwh7H7BRBBEiwAPXjadhhTRH-NwyOM-38ISiQtQySd6w42q9LJduDdmUKUhJnsjh6oUXx4VRoCn2gQAvD_BwE

"About Voice Forward & Anna Garduño." Accessed August 30, 2020. http://voiceforward.com/about/

"ACX." Accessed November 27, 2020. https://www.acx.com/

Gravy For The Brain. "ADR Voice Over Jobs - Find Out All About How To Get ADR Work." Accessed August 25, 2020. https://www.gravyforthebrain.com/adr-voice-over-jobs/

"Anime Voice Over Jobs - Find How To Get Into Anime Voice Over." Accessed August 25, 2020. https://www.gravyforthebrain.com/anime-voice-over-jobs/

"As Audiobook Market Grows, Narrators of Color Find Their Voice - The New York Times." Accessed November 1, 2020. https://www.nytimes.com/2020/06/03/books/audiobook-narrators-diversity.html

"Audacity Manual." Accessed October 8, 2020. https://manual.audacityteam.org/

"Audiobooks Featuring Must-Listen Performances | Audible.Com." Accessed September 8, 2020. https://www.audible.com/ep/best-performances-audiobooks

"Audiobooks Market Size, Share | Industry Report, 2020-2027." Accessed November 1, 2020. https://www.grandviewresearch.com/industry-analysis/audiobooks-market

Gravy For The Brain. "Audiobooks Voice Over Jobs - Find Out All About Audiobook Narration." Accessed September 4, 2020. https://www.gravyforthebrain.com/audiobook-voice-over-jobs/

"Best PBS Cartoons | List of Animated Kids Shows on PBS." Accessed September 13, 2020. https://www.ranker.com/list/best-pbs-cartoons/ranker-tv

"Breaking into the World of Video Game Voiceover." Accessed September 4, 2020. https://www.backstage.com/uk/magazine/article/breaking-world-video-game-voiceover-321/

Cobb, Michele. "Audiobooks continue their market rise with 16% growth in sales," n.d., 2.

"Copy Reading. How Do Voice Actors Make the Narration Pop? Voice Acting Coach Rachel Alena Dishes…" Accessed September 17, 2020. https://www.rachelalena.com/2017/05/01/voice-acting-coach-2/

"Create a Website with Weebly's Powerful Website Builder." Accessed October 11, 2020. https://www.weebly.com/websites

"Diction in Voiceover – The Voice Realm." Accessed September 17, 2020. https://www.thevoicerealm.com/blog/diction-in-voiceover/

"Do I Need An Agent For Voice Over Work? | Voquent." Accessed October 13, 2020. https://www.voquent.com/do-i-need-an-agent-for-voice-over-work/

"Do You Need a Voiceover Agent? | The Voiceover Gurus." Accessed October 13, 2020. https://voiceover.guru/do-you-need-a-voiceover-agent/

"Everything You Need to Know About Promo Voiceover Work." Accessed September 9, 2020. https://www.backstage.com/magazine/article/everything-need-know-promo-voiceover-work-1938/

"Fan of 'The Simpsons'? Audition for These Animated Projects." Accessed September 13, 2020. https://www.backstage.com/magazine/article/the-simpsons-fox-animation-casting-auditions-gigs-71700/?utm_campaign=Daily%20Jobs%20National&utm_medium=email&_hsmi=95092700&_hsenc=p2ANqtz--IhDAbHQK_qIovwjkrn4NcfTOEiy-ft4p--8fTnTScqJvCLqOCn03adJu8ui3QeHwssK9dGqzGS90Zvb-j0nnLtt2RpQ&utm_content=95092700&utm_source=hs_email

"Find Voice-Over Work & Voice Acting Jobs (Ultimate Guide)." Accessed October 13, 2020. https://voiceacting101.com/voice-over-work/

"Finding + Landing a Voiceover Agent." Accessed October 13, 2020. https://www.backstage.com/magazine/article/finding-landing-voiceover-agent-1063/

"Finding the Natural Rhythm in Voiceover Copy - Peter Drew Voiceovers." Accessed September 16, 2020. http://www.peterdrewvo.com/articles/finding-the-natural-rhythm-in-voiceover-copy/

"Free Voice Over Scripts - Read, Print & Practice Ready Voice Acting Scripts." Accessed October 11, 2020. https://www.voiceactorwebsites.com/free-voice-over-scripts/

"GarageBand for Windows 10 PC - Download & Install [2020]." Accessed October 8, 2020. https://garagebandforpcwindows.com/

"Getting a Voice Talent Agent | Voices.Com." Accessed October 13, 2020. https://www.voices.com/help/beginners-guide-to-voice-acting/getting-an-agent

"Getting an Agent – I Want to Be A Voice Actor!" Accessed October 13, 2020. https://iwanttobeavoiceactor.com/getting-an-agent/

"Glossary - Audacity Manual." Accessed October 8, 2020. https://manual.audacityteam.org/man/glossary.html

"Glossary of Voice Acting Terms | Global Voice Acting Academy | Voice Over Coaching & Classes." Accessed September 16, 2020. https://globalvoiceacademy.com/resources/glossary-of-voice-acting-terms/

"Glossary of Voiceover Terms All Actors Should Know." Accessed October 15, 2020. https://www.backstage.com/magazine/article/must-know-voiceover-terms-7216/

"Grammy-Winning Violinist Joshua Bell Delights Masses at DC Subway Concert | PBS NewsHour." Accessed August 26, 2020. https://www.pbs.org/newshour/arts/grammy-winning-violinist-joshua-bell-takes-another-turn-at-a-subway-concert

"GVAA Rate Guide | Global Voice Acting Academy | Voice Over Coaching & Classes." Accessed October 14, 2020. https://globalvoiceacademy.com/gvaa-rate-guide-2/

HAGEN, UTA, FRANKEL, HASKEL, & MASTERS, ANGELE. (2014). Respect for Acting. Brilliance Audio., n.d.

"How Much Do Voice Actors Make - Factors You Need To Know." Accessed October 29, 2020. https://www.gravyforthebrain.com/how-much-do-voice-actors-make/

"How Much Money Does a Voice Actor Make? | Beginners Guide to Voice Acting | Voices.Com." Accessed November 22, 2020. https://www.voices.com/help/beginners-guide-to-voice-acting/making-money-doing-voice-overs

"How to Be a Video Game Voiceover Artist." Accessed September 4, 2020. https://www.backstage.com/magazine/article/video-game-voiceover-artist-5572/

"How to Find a Great Voiceover Coach." Accessed September 22, 2020. https://www.backstage.com/magazine/article/how-to-find-a-great-voiceover-coach-66201/

"How To Find And Hire A Voice Actor Online | Voice Over Website." Accessed October 11, 2020. https://www.thevoicerealm.com/how-to-hire-voice-actors.php

"How to Find Voiceover Work in E-Learning, Corporate Narration, Audiobooks + Explainer Videos." Accessed September 9, 2020. https://www.backstage.com/magazine/article/voiceover-e-learning-corporate-narration-audiobooks-explainers-68726/

"How To Get a Voice Agent - Tips from a Top Voice Agent." Accessed October 13, 2020. https://www.gravyforthebrain.com/how-to-get-a-voice-agent/

"How To Make A Voice-Over Demo." Accessed October 11, 2020. https://www.suchavoice.com/2017/06/09/howtomakeavoiccoverdemo/

"How to Master Voiceover Character Skills." Accessed September 7, 2020. https://usa.gravyforthebrain.com/how-to-master-voiceover-character-skills/

"How to Talk to Samuel L. Jackson Using Alexa | Digital Trends." Accessed February 15, 2021. https://www.digitaltrends.com/home/how-to-talk-to-samuel-l-jackson-using-alexa/

"How To Use GarageBand on a Mac - Easy Tips & Pointers | Voices.Com." Accessed October 8, 2020. https://www.voices.com/blog/getting_started_with_garageband/

"How Voice Actors Are Fighting Whitewashing in Animation - Vox." Accessed October 30, 2020. https://www.vox.com/2020/7/22/21326824/white-voice-actors-black-characters-cartoons-whitewashing

https://www.facebook.com/ToddCFrankel. "In $25 Billion Video Game Industry, Voice Actors Face Broken Vocal Cords and Low Pay." Washington Post. Accessed October 30, 2020. https://www.washingtonpost.com/business/economy/in-24-billion-video-game-industry-voice-actors-dont-make-enough-to-live-on/2017/10/27/944a0800-98d8-11e7-87fc-c3f7ee4035c9_story.html

"IVR Voice Over Jobs - Create An Income By Voicing IVR." Accessed August 25, 2020. https://www.gravyforthebrain.com/ivr-voice-over-jobs/

"Looping and ADR - Bonnie Gillespie." Accessed September 10, 2020. https://bonniegillespie.com/looping-and-adr/

"Merle Dandridge | Official Website." Accessed February 4, 2021. https://www.merledandridge.com/voiceover.html

"Movie Trailer Mastery | Complete Voiceover." Accessed December 5, 2020. https://complete-voiceover.com/movie-trailer-mastery/

"Movie Trailer Voices - Best Voice Overs [Audio] | Voices.Com." Accessed February 15, 2021. https://www.voices.com/voice-actors/style/movie-trailer

"Pattern Interruption And The Musicality Of Voice Over - Vo2gogo.Com." Accessed September 17, 2020. https://www.vo2gogo.com/pattern-interruption-and-the-musicality-of-voice-over/

"Pitch: Public Speaking/Speech Communication." Accessed September 15, 2020. https://lumen.instructure.com/courses/218897/pages/linkedtext54274

"Planning Your Voice-Over Demos | Voices.Com." Accessed October 9, 2020. https://www.voices.com/help/beginners-guide-to-voice-acting/planning-your-demos

"Podcast Voice Overs - Pro Podcast Solutions." Accessed September 4, 2020. https://propodcastsolutions.com/podcast-voice-overs/

Preston, Marc. "How to Choose a Reputable Voiceover Coach/Consultant," n.d. https://marcprestonconsulting.com/choosingacoach/

"Read This Before You Hire a Voice Over Coach - Bunny Studio." Accessed September 22, 2020. https://bunnystudio.com/blog/read-this-before-you-hire-a-voice-over-coach/

"Reading a Script | Voice Over Tips & Resources — The Voice Shop." Accessed September 17, 2020. http://www.voiceshopcoaching.com/reading-a-script

"Search Voice Actors By Voice Over Category | Voices.Com." Accessed October 11, 2020. https://www.voices.com/voice-actors/category

Siegel, Cecelia. *VoiceOver Achiever: Brand Your VO Career. Change Your Life.* Celia Siegel (January 15, 2018), n.d.

"Some Voice Over Film Examples for Your Entertainment - Bunny Studio." Accessed September 11, 2020. https://bunnystudio.com/blog/some-voice-over-film-examples-for-your-entertainment/

"Speed Reading - Why Voiceovers Need To Master This Art." Accessed September 10, 2020. https://usa.gravyforthebrain.com/the-art-of-speed-reading/

"Susan Bennett - Wikipedia." Accessed February 15, 2021. https://en.wikipedia.org/wiki/Susan_Bennett

"Talking Pen Point Reading Pen For Educational Kids And Students - Buy Electronic Talking Pen,Educational English Book With Talking Pen,Kids Fancy Story Pens Product on Alibaba.Com." Accessed February 15, 2021. https://www.alibaba.com/product-detail/talking-pen-point-reading-pen-for_60723414040.html?spm=a2700.7724857.normal_offer.d_image.790a1764MSo7TD&s=p&fullFirstScreen=true

"Talking Products | LS&S, LLC." Accessed February 15, 2021. https://lssproducts.com/talking-products/

"The 4 Most Important Elements Of Your Voice." Accessed September 16, 2020. https://www.fastcompany.com/3047183/the-4-most-important-elements-of-your-voice

"The Art of Voice-Over Cadences - Such A Voice." Accessed September 16, 2020. https://www.suchavoice.com/2019/03/07/the-art-of-voice-over-cadences/

"The Best Audible Books in 2020 | TechRadar." Accessed November 2, 2020. https://www.techradar.com/best/best-audible-books

"The Best Audio Editing Software for 2020 | PCMag." Accessed October 8, 2020. https://www.pcmag.com/picks/the-best-audio-editing-software?test_uuid=01jrZgWNXhmA3ocG7ZHXevj&test_variant=b

"The Best Black Audiobook Narrators to Listen To Right Now | Audible.Com." Accessed November 2, 2020. https://www.audible.com/blog/playlisted/article-best-black-audiobook-narrators-to-listen-to?ref=a_ep_best-p_bsn_md_subHeading_1_0

"The Complete Guide to Improving Vocal Control - Ramsey Voice Studio." Accessed September 17, 2020. https://ramseyvoice.com/vocal-control/

"The Importance of IVR Phone System Voice Over | Voices.Com Blog." Accessed August 26, 2020. https://www.voices.com/blog/telephone-system-voice-over/

Thompson, Stuart A. "In a World without Voiceovers: What Happened to the Movie Trailer Voice?" The Globe and Mail, May 22, 2014. https://www.theglobeandmail.com/arts/film/in-a-world-without-voiceovers-what-happened-to-the-movie-trailer-voice/article18806436/

"Top 10 Audio Recording Software to Capture Your Voice Easily." Accessed October 8, 2020. https://filmora.wondershare.com/best-audio-recording-software.html

"Types of Vocal Timbre | Music To Your Home." Accessed September 19, 2020. https://www.musictoyourhome.com/blog/types-of-vocal-timbre/

"Videos | Audiobook Creation Exchange Blog (ACX)." Accessed September 4, 2020. https://blog.acx.com/category/videos/

Voice Acting Academy. "Get Started in Voiceover," n.d. https://voiceacting.com/training/get-started-in-voiceover/

"Voice Matching in Movies - Business Insider." Accessed December 7, 2020. https://www.businessinsider.com/voice-matching-in-movies-2016-3

"Voice Over Business - How To Create A Thriving VO Business." Accessed October 13, 2020. https://www.gravyforthebrain.com/start-voice-over-business/

"Voice Over Demo Scripts: Everything You Need to Know." Accessed September 24, 2020. https://bunnystudio.com/blog/voice-over-demo-scripts-everything-you-need-to-know/

"Voice Over Gurus Blog | The Online VoiceOver Community." Accessed September 16, 2020. http://www.voiceovergurus.com/guru_blog/

"Voice Over Sample Scripts | Edge Studio." Accessed October 11, 2020. https://www.edgestudio.com/voice-over-scripts

"Voice Over Trends in 2020 and Why Voice Over Coaching Remains More Important Than Ever." Accessed October 30, 2020. https://wp.nyu.edu/dispatch/2020/03/20/voice-over-trends-in-2020-and-why-voice-over-coaching-remains-more-important-than-ever/

"Voiceoverview - Voice Over CRM and Voice Actor Business Management Tool." Accessed October 14, 2020. https://voiceoverview.com/

"VoiceOverXtra: \'I Am Not A Black Voice Actor. I Am Not An African-American Voice Actor. I Am A Voice Actor \'- Kabir Singh." Accessed February 15, 2021. https://www.voiceoverxtra.com/article.htm?id=UBPRUUXQ

"Weebly Pricing - Compare Website Builder Plans and Pricing." Accessed October 11, 2020. https://www.weebly.com/pricing

"What Are the Payments for Cable Use? | SAG-AFTRA." Accessed October 23, 2020. https://www.sagaftra.org/what-are-payments-cable-use

"What Is a Preamplifier? Why Do We Need Them? | LedgerNote." Accessed February 15, 2021. https://ledgernote.com/columns/studio-recording/what-is-a-preamplifier/

"What It's Like to Work on Video Games, According to 'Mass Effect' VO Actor Jennifer Hale." Accessed September 7, 2020. https://www.backstage.com/magazine/article/act-video-games-jennifer-hale-mass-effect-43991/

"What Voice Actors Need to Know About 'Voice Matching.'" Accessed September 4, 2020. https://www.backstage.com/magazinc/article/match-game-1 63931/

"What Voice Actors Should Know About Looping, ADR + Walla." Accessed September 10, 2020. https://www.backstage.com/magazine/article/what-voice-actors-should-know-about-looping-adr-walla-69048/

"What's ADR in Film and Why Is It Important?" Accessed August 26, 2020. https://nofilmschool.com/what-is-adr-in-film

"Who Is the Voice of Alexa?" Accessed February 15, 2021. https://www.muo.com/who-is-the-voice-of-alexa/

"Why Your Next Voiceover Job Is Probably in Your Phone." Accessed February 7, 2021. https://www.backstage.com/magazine/article/smart-gadgets-siri-voiceover-work-66209/

Wix Pricing Information | Upgrade to a Premium Plan | Wix.com. "Wix Pricing Information | Upgrade to a Premium Plan | Wix.Com." Accessed October 11, 2020. https://www.wix.com/upgrade/website

"Women Narrate Movie Trailers | Industry News - Celebrities | Voices.Com Blog." Accessed September 22, 2020. https://www.voices.com/blog/in_a_world_where_women_narrate_movie_trailers/

WonderConBornJune 15, Fred TatascioreTatasciore at the 2018, 1967New York City, and U. S. OccupationVoice actorYears active1999–present. "Fred Tatasciore - Wikipedia." Accessed September 16, 2020. https://en.wikipedia.org/wiki/Fred_Tatasciore